ROYCE HALL

ROYCE HALL

JAMES KLAIN
ARNOLD J. BAND

Edited
by
CHANDLER HARRIS

Designed
by
JACK CARTER

University of California, Los Angeles

Frontispiece: Josiah Royce

FOREWORD

Royce Hall, a unique campus building, was one of the first structures at UCLA. In its more than fifty years, it has become the sentimental home of thousands of alumni and the recognized center of a cultural program of the finest performing arts the world has to offer. The twin Romanesque towers of Royce, separated by their peaked loggia, present a graphic outline which has become identifiable in far corners of the earth. It is the symbol of UCLA.

The closing of Royce for renovation provided an occasion to take a retrospective look at the building and its significance to students, staff and faculty and to assess the impact of its programs and activities on the cultural life of the broader community. This book is the result.

In addition to recounting the genesis and history of Royce, the authors and designer have assembled a wealth of illustration of the building in whole and in detail, and we are indebted to them for a handsome record of UCLA's best-loved and best-known structure.

The aspiration of UCLA's founders are reflected in the nature of the decorations they chose for the foyer and loggias of the building and the stained glass windows of the stairways. Time has dimmed the colors of some of the murals, and others, located on ceilings which are difficult to access, have been carefully photographed and reproduced in this volume.

Throughout this volume have been woven photographs of the various symbols selected by the founders to represent academic inspiration and intellectual achievement. Among these are the seals of twelve of the great universities of Europe and medallions of the twelve professions of early Western culture, together with the names of leaders in each field, a total of ninety-four historic figures. Quotations from some of these outstanding intellectuals (to be found on the ceiling of the third floor loggia) also appear. In addition, there are reproductions of the beautiful stained glass windows illustrating the endeavors and activities of a great university. This publication thus preserves the symbols which were intended to serve as daily reminders to students of the great mission of the university, past and present.

Charles E. Young
Chancellor

ACKNOWLEDGEMENTS

A publication such as this involves the effort and encouragement of a great many people in order to be brought to fruition. *Royce Hall* is no exception. The initial inspiration and concept for this book was that of Vice Chancellor Elwin V. Svenson. He charted the dimensions of our work and step by step enthusiastically encouraged and focused our energies. He provided each of us with a unique vision of Royce Hall, not just a structure of brick, concrete, plaster and glass, but a Royce Hall that serves as the ever-present symbol of a university of truly unique character and quality. His luggage, on his university missions throughout the world during the past year, has been weighted down with the successive rewrites of the manuscript as the book has metamorphosed. His judgment of the process of creating a work such as this has provided the benchmark for its orderly development.

We wish to thank Executive Vice Chancellor William Schaefer for his advice, encouragement, and critical eye in periodically reviewing this work in progress. Professor Richard Kent Nystrom's comprehensive work on UCLA was a uniquely valuable resource.

There have been many others who have assisted greatly in various aspects of this book who should be mentioned. We are indebted to the artistry and taste of Norman Schindler and Terry O'Donnell of the ASUCLA Photography Studio, Howard Tribe and Philip Bleicher of the Office of Instructional Development photographic service, John Gaylord, Dr. David Palmer, John Jackson, Thelner Hoover, Tom Feldman, Otto Rothschild, Stan Troutman, Pete Saloutos, UCLA Library Photographic Service, and many unknown staff photographers of past editions of the Southern Campus and other contributors to the photographic collections of the UCLA Library Archives for some truly outstanding as well as historically important photographs.

For giving of their time and energy to share their UCLA experience over past years and adding to the lore of Royce Hall we are indebted to William Ackerman, David Allison, Dean Gustave Arlt, Professor Leonard Freedman, Professor Ralph Freud, Professor Thomas Harmon, Professor Thomas Hines, John Jackson, Professor Jack Morrison, Dean Charles Speroni, Thomas Stead, and Ann Sumner. We are also indebted to the following for their encouragement, advice, and technical expertise in various facets of this book's preparation: Sidney Kahn, Thomas Tugend, and Pebbles Wadsworth.

We are grateful for the resources made available to us by the UCLA Library Department of Special Collections (Hilda Bohem), the UCLA Library University Archives (Ann Caiger and Dan Luckenbill), the Associated Students collection of Southern Campus publications and the California Historical Society. Also to be thanked are the Harvard University Archives for the use of some rare historic photographic materials, Dennis Dee, and the resource references of Steven Sann.

And lastly, to the staff of the Office of Institutional Relations: Dana Farrington, Que Gatlin, Nancy Lumsden and others for their Olympian patience and service and advice.

James Klain
Arnold J. Band

ON A CLEAR DAY

The photographs taken of Royce Hall upon its completion in 1929 are often a source of amazement. What, one asks, was this imposing building doing in the middle of a sheep pasture? Close-ups of the carefully wrought features, the graceful, arched colonnade topped by two soaring towers, so perfectly balanced despite their deliberate difference of detail, signify the style: northern Italian Romanesque. What, one wonders, was a massive Romanesque structure doing in the rolling hills of Los Angeles, close to the very end of the continent, close enough, in fact, to permit a distant view of the Pacific Ocean? The proximity of nearby Hollywood might lead to the conjecture that the building was a set, a stucco and canvas facade masquerading as an architectural gem of the Middle Ages. But early aerial photographs reveal that Royce Hall was real indeed, the center-piece of a little cluster of buildings in the same Lombardian style.

One might expect to find such a building in the midst of a crowded Mediterranean city, with its centuries of architectural accumulation—all evidence of a long history of human culture. It is only on learning that Royce Hall was designed to be the center of a new university campus that one understands the mission of its architecture—it was chosen to express kinship with the great academic tradition of the leading European universities, a breath of Lombardy in the hills of Westwood.

The University's founders and its architects made a fortunate choice in selecting Romanesque over the many other Italian architectural styles which might also have commented on the similarity in climate and landscape between Italy and Los Angeles. Roman-

esque, they knew, was the attempt of medieval people to fashion buildings and works of art resembling the ruined artifacts of the earlier Roman civilization. Utilizing local materials and talent, medieval builders progressed from initially crude to ultimately elegant edifices which alluded to the vanished glory of Rome while giving full expression to their own temper and vision. Their reverence for the past was not slavish or inhibiting; on the contrary, it sustained their imagination and gave it shape.

Royce Hall's architects—in both the figurative and literal sense—found in the Romanesque style the embodiment of their vision. They determined to build in the open fields of Westwood a university which would pay tribute both architecturally and academically to the institutions which sustained the

Site of the Westwood campus showing the approximate campus boundaries overlaid on the photograph.

UCLA campus view, about 1930.

spirit of learning over many centuries; Romanesque offered an appropriate setting for a university engaged in disseminating the rich cultural heritage of the past as well as creating new knowledge for future generations.

No one can say whether it was luck or simply intimacy with Italian structures which led the architects to model Royce Hall after Milan's San Ambrogio, constructed in the tenth and eleventh centuries. The happy result was a building at once grand and graceful, with a facade entirely worthy of symbolizing the prominent institution which UCLA would one day become. At the time Royce Hall was built, it was hard to foresee that the inconspicuous regional school to be housed there would in such a short time rise to a place among the leaders of American higher education. Its potential, however, was already apparent to the first provost, Ernest Carroll Moore; ten years earlier he had predicted that the university was "certain to be greater, far greater than the imagination of any of us can foresee."

As if in preparation for that dimly imagined future, Moore reinforced the symbolism of Royce's architecture by decorating the foyer with seals of the great universities of Europe, from Oxford to Heidelberg. Thus Royce Hall, the first building on the UCLA campus, was from the beginning a statement in brick and stone of a challenge which might take years or even centuries to realize. After all, many of the institutions whose seals appear on the foyer ceiling were founded five or six centuries before ground was broken in the pastures of Westwood.

It is unlikely that even Provost Moore could have guessed that his vision of the University's future would materialize during the lifetime of the first students to attend classes in Royce Hall. It is also remarkable that the facade of Royce Hall has so quickly become a recognized symbol of academic achievement. The seemingly quixotic dreams of the architects have been overtaken by the reality of the present.

The newly completed Royce Hall.

San Ambrogio Church, Milan. The arch designs were transmitted to Royce Hall by architect David Allison.

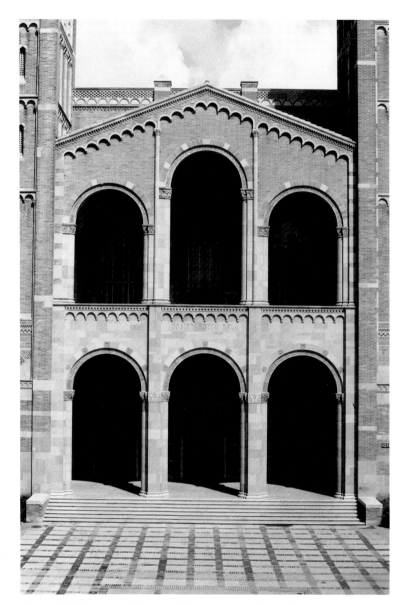

Royce Hall, an architectural inspiration from the Romanesque.

TRANSPLANTING
A 700-YEAR-OLD TRADITION

When the film version of Maxwell Anderson's *Winterset* was released in 1936, it contained a background photograph of Royce Hall identified as an Eastern law school. Because Royce Hall has become the widely recognized symbol of UCLA itself, University officials would not permit such a fictional film use of the building today, and in any event it would likely provoke unplanned laughter from a knowledgeable audience. The growth of UCLA and of public familiarity with Royce Hall's distinctive silhouette has a short but lively history and one which involves many diverse figures and forces. Among them are UCLA's determined founders, the recognition by thousands of citizens of the need for quality public education in Southern California, the dedication of faculty and administrators to filling that need, the long and continuing presentation of outstanding cultural events to the public on the Royce Hall stage, and the increasing use of the Royce Hall symbol not only to signify the best in artistic presentations but to stand for the University itself and the academic eminence it has achieved.

The events which led to UCLA's academic and public recognition began in 1917 when Ernest Carroll Moore was called from Harvard to head the Los Angeles State Normal School, a two-year institution with an enrollment of 1,671 prospective teachers. In the hope of converting the school to a four-year teacher's college, Moore joined forces with Edward A. Dickson, a Los Angeles newspaper editor who was the youngest member of the University of California's Board of Regents and the only one from Southern

California. It was Dickson's dream to establish a Los Angeles branch of the University of California to meet the region's growing need for public higher education.

The two men were an unusual combination: Moore, the philosopher and educator with a touch of scholarly diffidence, and Dickson, the practical executive with the natural instincts of a crusader. However different their personalities, they formed an effective team as they worked their way patiently through the many twists and turns of state and university policy and politics. Against heavy opposition from the northern part of the state, they achieved the assimilation of the normal school into the

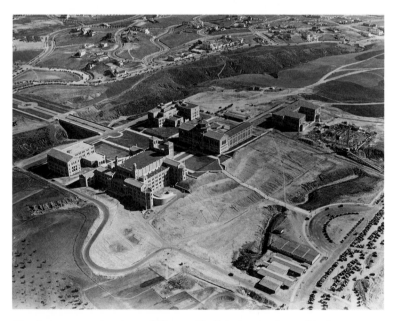

Early panoramic view of Royce Hall prior to the softening of the building's outlines by the growth of trees and bushes.

12

David Allison, architect of Royce Hall. His work in the design of the buildings on the Vermont Avenue campus prompted his selection by Moore to design Royce Hall. He had taken the leadership to encourage and expand the use of brick as a building material in Southern California.

Edward A. Dickson, publisher and former student of Moore's at Berkeley. He aspired to service only as a member of the Board of Regents as a reward for his political service. But for his diligence and perseverance, the development of UCLA might have been delayed for decades.

Ernest Carroll Moore, first Provost (and Vice President of the University of California) at UCLA. He was a well-known educator and educational philosopher who set the high goals and aspirations for the new university in its formative years.

University of California as a two-year "Southern Branch" in 1919, followed by a four-year teachers college curriculum in 1922 and a four-year letters and science curriculum in 1924. The name of the campus was changed to the University of California at Los Angeles in 1927 (the "at" was replaced by a comma in 1958).

Not too many years into the 1920s it became apparent that the University's midtown campus on Vermont Avenue was already inadequate for the growing institution and much too small for future development. A new location was sought by a representative committee of local citizens, and after a study of 19 possible sites, the Westwood Hills property was selected. UCLA students, staff and faculty combined with citizen groups to carry out successful bond issue campaigns in the cities of Los Angeles, Beverly Hills, Santa Monica and Venice in order to buy the property and present it to the Regents as a gift.

By 1925, the Regents were able to instruct the University Architect to start overall campus planning. Moore wanted a local architect included in the process, and he selected Allison and Allison, the firm which had designed the buildings on the Vermont Avenue campus as well as several other Los Angeles structures of artistic worth. David Allison, who is believed to have suggested the Romanesque style for the new campus, was given the assignment of designing the building which was to become Royce Hall.

Allison loved the Lombardic form of Romanesque found in northern Italy and he also loved the colors and textures of brick, a material used extensively by the Lombards. Moore was in complete agreement with these plans, not only because the

San Ambrogio Church. The warm brick tones so common in the Lombardic Romanesque style lent themselves to the Southern California ambiance of Royce Hall.

Early (1926) master plan for UCLA by George Kelham, University Architect. He was the building architect for Powell Library and Haines Hall as well as overall supervising architect in the early phases of the Westwood campus building program.

14

warm brick exteriors would "always be vital as the sun plays upon them" but because Romanesque, an architectural representation of the earliest recovery from the Dark Ages, was contemporary with the founding of such historic Italian universities as Bologna (1088) and Padua (1222). The forms and intricacies of Lombardic Romanesque seemed ideally suited to the site, climate, geography and purpose of the new UCLA campus.

In developing the plans for Royce Hall, Moore and Allison were aware that they were creating a building whose brick and concrete might last two thousand years and whose academic symbolism would speak to many generations of the campus community. To accomplish its mission, Royce must be impressive, beautiful and eloquent. Moreover, there were practical considerations which could not be overlooked concerning the functions which the building would serve. As the campus would open with only four permanent structures in place, Royce Hall needed to be much more than an auditorium; the academic requirements of the young university called for lecture halls of various sizes as well as faculty and departmental offices. Since the auditorium would be the site of public lectures, ceremonies and performances, it would serve both the academic and public communities, providing an intimate intermingling of town and gown as in the medieval universities.

The solution to providing for these differing needs was a building within a building, which is what Royce actually is. The inner building consists of an auditorium and its supplemental spaces, from foyer to backstage. The outer building includes smaller lecture halls, classrooms and faculty offices. To create such a structure with the required space and flexibility, the architects departed from the conventional box within a box to something more imaginative—the Romanesque cathedral, a complex of buildings held together by an overall vision of society. Hence the wings, the colonnade, the towers and the variegated geometric shapes—all fused into a harmony of disparate parts. From the plurality of uses, one magnificent edifice arose.

Following San Ambrogio's best features closely, Allison selected the two square towers framing the central arches, then added a wing on either side, thus disguising the massiveness of the structure behind a graceful facade. Over the reinforced concrete of the building's skeleton, he applied a brick shell which offers a remarkable display of the mason's artistry, employing the entire spectrum of 19 colors of brick then available. He decorated the shell with inlays, cast stone and terra cotta and embellished the wings with handsome loggias.

Taking a vaulting from one Romanesque model, developing it like a variation on a theme and placing it over a porch element from another Lombardian example, Allison created his own architectural masterpiece. The result was a building of which any university could be proud, a building with strong roots in the academic past which continued to speak movingly to scholars of the present.

The structure carried a second and more subtle message; it was completely different from anything on the "mother" campus at Berkeley. While the prestige granted by UCLA's affiliation with the University of California was fully appreciated, there was also a strong desire to establish an independent identity

Architect David Allison's presentation drawing of the proposed Royce Hall.

The south, Quad, side of Royce.

The southeast corner of Royce as the brick and terra-cotta finishes are applied.

The west side of Royce.

The west side as the brick veneer is completed.

A view of Royce from the northeast corner.

Workmen installing one of the ceiling coffers over the auditorium.

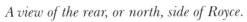

A view of the rear, or north, side of Royce.

The auditorium interior under construction.

The northeast loggia. Ceiling decoration was another important element of the Romanesque in Royce.

The well-known south, or front, loggia in a view familiar to thousands of concertgoers.

A view showing the intricacy of detail in Royce Hall's many faces.

Typical complex brickwork and inserts as seen at the base of the west tower. Asymmetry and decorative variation were hallmarks of the Lombardic Romanesque style.

for the Los Angeles campus. Royce Hall and its little group of Romanesque buildings resembled nothing else in the state system.

The Lombardian custom of painting the ceilings of public structures offered another opportunity to emphasize the academic heritage of the new campus. When Allison asked what should be painted on the ceilings of Royce's loggias, Moore offered the following suggestion:

"Why not paint the Instruction of the World? Start with Socrates, and opposite Socrates paint the figure of the Christ, and on their right hand and their left hand paint their chief disciples, for they happen to have been the same men, Plato and Aristotle. There you have your ancient world. Now, fortunately for us as we have three arches, human history has three parts. For the medieval period start with Abelard, the father of the universities; opposite him paint Petrarch, the prime mover of the Renaissance, and on their right hand and their left hand paint Melanchthon, the schoolmaster general of the Reformation, and Loyola, the director of the Counter Reformation. There you have the great shaping forces of the Middle Ages.

"When we come to modern times, the going is harder. But begin with Immanuel Kant; and there was a man in England named Charles Darwin. Paint him opposite Immanuel Kant. From our own country take that man who did the most to change the character of universities and teaching in general, both in our own country and beyond the United States, Charles W. Eliot; and, lest the young people who come here may think that these are just names of men who never lived at all, take one living man, the greatest of living scientists, Albert Einstein."

An architectural detail along the south loggia.

A 1940 campus view. The streets bounding the campus received their names by the placement on the proposed plot map of the names of favorite Berkeley professors of the time: Hilgard, LeConte, and Gayley. It was assumed by the Berkeley staff who prepared the plans that the names would be changed by Los Angeles city authorities during the plan-approval process. However, they were approved as submitted.

The southwest corner.

A unique night view of the south loggia showing the decorated ceilings.

The passageway familiar to Royce audiences. Each quadrant of the vaulting has a stylized depiction of one of the twelve medieval professions. Along the base of each quadrant are listed the names of famed practitioners of that profession.

Symbolic representations of these men became the ceiling decorations of the third floor loggia; for the first floor loggia Moore prescribed representations of twelve professions, with a listing of the names of the great practitioners of the following disciplines: Graphic Arts, Education, Language, Biology, History, Mathematics, Literature-Drama, Philosophy, Chemistry, Music, Physics and Astronomy. (See page 111 for quotations from the ceiling and names of the twelve professions.)

The inscriptions over the doors leading to the classroom corridors were also from sources Moore admired; one came from Royce, the other from Plato. Feeling that Royce should be represented directly on the building which was to bear his name, Moore chose this quotation from Royce's *Problems of Christianity:* "The world is a progressively realized community of interpretation."

Reaching back to the philosopher that Moore felt was integral to all educational development, he chose Plato's admonition: "They should learn beforehand the knowledge which they will require for their art."

The inscription over the proscenium arch in the auditorium is pure Ernest Carroll Moore. Some years earlier Moore had been asked to provide an inscription for an arch in Millspaugh Hall on the Vermont Avenue campus of the Normal School. He had offered, "Education is learning to use the tools which the race has found indispensable." Architect Allison, wishing to bring some element of the old campus to the new, had ordered the inscription placed in Royce Hall without consulting Moore. Unfortunately, University protocol prescribed that such inscriptions

The window and inscription over the southeast door.

The window and inscription over the southwest door.

The center front door. Although the five front doors on the south side look similar at first glance, they are all different in architectural detail and embellishment—a further evidence of the wealth of care and design lavished on the building.

Intermission during the final performance in Royce prior to the remodeling in February 1983.

must be authorized by the University of California president, and President William W. Campbell strenuously objected. However, the inscription was already in concrete, and in spite of Campbell's objections and years of irreverent undergraduate paraphrasing, Moore's words remain.

It is appropriate that Moore should be remembered in Royce Hall as well as in the education building which was later renamed for him. It has often been observed that the quality of faculty built into the University during his administration provided a sound base for growth as the institution added graduate work and, later, its professional schools. Initial concerns for high standards of faculty selection played a part in setting UCLA on the pathway to its eventual academic ranking among the top half-dozen American universities.

The ceiling of the auditorium, representing the culmination of the architectural style of the building, was a complex of concave, square coffers, 72 in all, in light blue and gold. Each unit was hand cast and lacquered on the site and then raised and plastered into position. In addition to their beauty, the coffers provided an essential acoustical element: an attractive but irregular surface to disperse sound in a manner similar to the effect of the elaborate decor found in some of the finer nineteenth century concert halls in Europe. During the recent refurbishing of the auditorium, all the coffers were redecorated by hand.

A close-up view of one of Royce Hall's seventy-two ceiling coffers during the repainting as part of the renovation. Much of the gold decoration was highlighted by the application of gold leaf.

The ceiling, above, of the 8th century Church of Santa Maria
Maggiore in Rome shows a remarkable similarity to the Royce
Hall auditorium ceiling, below.

A close-up view of the newly decorated ceiling.

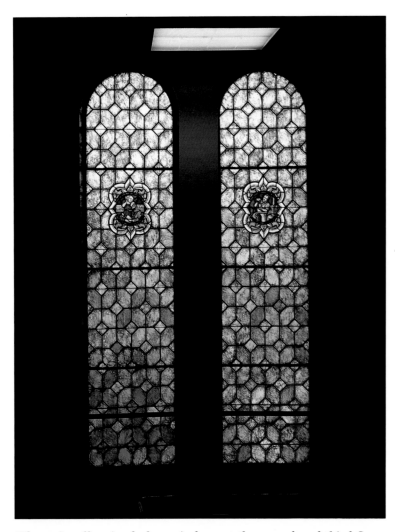

The stairwell stained glass windows at the second and third floor landings in each corner of the building.

A close-up view of one of the six stained glass windows. This one is a pictorial representation of chemistry.

In the stairwells of the building, the architect placed 15-foot-high stained glass windows with brightly colored inserts on the subjects of wisdom, the arts, mining and geological sciences, law and justice, science and chemistry, and the skill of sport. Stained glass windows were also placed within the auditorium itself in the walls above the balcony; they consisted of simple, pastel roundels of glass with no other panel or design. With the remodelling of the auditorium these were moved to the windows along the first floor loggia.

On the beams of the auditorium's outer lobby, through which thousands of citizens were destined to flow in the years to come, were depicted the seals of the great European universities: Bologna, Cambridge, Heidelberg, Leyden, Montpelier, Oxford, Padua, Paris, Prague, Salamanca, St. Andrews and Upsala. The youngest of these was founded in 1575; the oldest, in 1088. Individually and collectively they represented the foundation and growth of Western culture as expressed in university learning and were intended to provide a permanent reminder of the high levels of scholastic attainment to which the new university was dedicated. The seals also serve as a recognition of the role of universities as permanent centers of learning and exploration, outlasting duchies, baronies, governments, revolutions, and the ravages of war and pestilence.

Pastel Roundels of glass which may be seen on the lobby landing to the balcony and along the south loggia.

The seal of the University of St. Andrews

THE NAME AND THE MAN BEHIND IT

The naming of UCLA's symbolic structure for Josiah Royce came about through a series of curious connections. The choice was unusual because Royce, a Harvard professor, had never taught at UCLA. Still, Royce, the leading American idealist philosopher, had roots in the state and close ties to the founders of the new Los Angeles campus. A graduate of the University of California, Royce taught at Berkeley for a short period prior to receiving a permanent appointment to the Harvard University faculty.

As his career at Harvard progressed, Royce became increasingly famous for his lectures and publications. Although most of his work was in philosophy, he published an early novel and wrote a well-known history of California. Among his best-known publications are *The Religious Aspect of Philosophy, The Problem of Christianity, The Spirit of Modern Philosophy, The World and the Individual, Outlines of Psychology, The Philosophy of Loyalty,* and *The Sources of Religious Thought.*

He was lecturing in Berkeley when World War I began. The war created a great tension in Royce because of his strong emotional and intellectual ties to German philosophy and thought. However, after the sinking of the Lusitania, he became highly partisan, lecturing to his classes that the war's opponents were Germany and humanity. As he became obsessed with the war, his health progressively declined, and he died in 1916.

In spite of Royce's disillusion with Germany in wartime, his studies at leading universities there enabled him to join other scholars in bringing to American higher education the German academic goal: the role of the university in seeking truth rather than merely transmitting knowledge and culture from one generation to the next. This new concept led to a revolution in scientific inquiry, and universities became active leaders in research. The structure of higher education was permanently changed.

Ernest Carroll Moore had been a colleague of Royce's at Harvard, and his admiration for Royce was shared by Charles H. Reiber, who was to serve UCLA for many years as the first dean of the College of Letters and Science. Reiber had taken his graduate studies at Harvard under Royce and had taught philosophy before joining the UCLA administration.

During the months the new campus at Westwood was under construction, Moore and Reiber made many trips to observe its progress. On one of these visits, Reiber suggested that the new library be named for Royce. He reminded Moore of William James' famous characterization of his colleague, "Royce knows everything." Such a dedication would serve as an excellent model for the generations of students to come. Moore reflected for a time and replied, "His name will not be used if we attach it to the library. Let us ask the Regents instead to call our chief classroom building for him; then he will always be named whenever that building is referred to."

It was a gesture of real significance, particularly since there was no plan at the time to name any other building. For an individual to be so honored, it must be someone whose life and career exemplify the goals and aspirations of the institution. The choice was not that of a land developer, a generous contrib-

The newly remodeled "checkerboard" lobby showing the location of the seals on the ceiling beams.

utor, a local hero or even a revered teacher. It was a choice symbolizing UCLA's desire to carry on the best traditions of Western culture and scholarship.

The choice, however, was not without a tinge of irony, since Californian admiration for Royce was not wholeheartedly reciprocated. Royce had referred to California as "this sad state wherein I had the odd fortune to be born," and Mrs. Royce had presaged Gertrude Stein's well-known characterization of Oak-

land with her description of Grass Valley as "a place that was nothing in a situation that was nowhere." Moreover, Royce had told William James that California was a philosophically barren area. Nevertheless, Royce was undeniably a product of the University of California, and had he known that his name would be given to a building which would eventually be world famous in artistic circles, he might have taken a kinder view of his native state.

A rear view of the west tower.

The northeast corner tower which housed the smokestack for the sub-basement boiler room before the boilers were moved to the south campus area.

Josiah Royce, born in 1855 in Grass Valley, California, of parents who had come to the United States from England. He enrolled, at age 15, in the fourth freshman class at the new University of California in Oakland (the campus moved to Berkeley in 1873). He earned his Bachelor of Arts degree in 1875 at the age of 19. He then went to Germany to study at Leipzig and Göttingen before returning to a graduate teaching position at Johns Hopkins University, where he received his Ph.D. degree.

During a four-year period of teaching English at the University of California, he met Katherine Head, daughter of a prominent San Francisco attorney; they were married in 1880. Two years later, after the birth of their first child, Royce accepted a year's appointment to Harvard. At first, he was only a sabbatical replacement for William James, and for a few years he served as a temporary replacement for various Harvard faculty members on leave. But in 1885 he received a permanent professorial appointment.

The northwest corner tower.

EDUCATION IS LEARNING TO USE THE TOOLS WHICH THE RACE HAS FOUND INDISPENSABLE

Although Royce Hall is best known to the wider public as the home of performances by leading artists in every field, in the early years it was as Provost Moore characterized it: UCLA's chief classroom building. It was particularly the site of the humanities—the classics, literature and languages, history and philosophy—but its classrooms were also used by many other disciplines. Even the auditorium was pressed into use during the first years, housing classes in music, psychology, philosophy and education. During its lifetime Royce has provided space for many academic offices, including at various periods such departments as African Studies, Business Administration, the College of Applied Arts, Comparative Literature, Communication Studies, Economics, English, Nursing, Political Science, and Speech, in addition to the previously mentioned subjects. Many departments still have their headquarters in the building.

At first, Royce also sheltered a few administrative offices, including the deans of men and women, the offices of student government, and such activities as the student newspaper and yearbook.

At the time Royce Hall was built, its auditorium (with a capacity of nearly 2,000) could seat a large part of the student body, and many convocations called by the provost were held there. The auditorium also served an educational purpose with numerous public lectures and ceremonies to which students were invited.

Records indicate that the earliest celebrated fig-

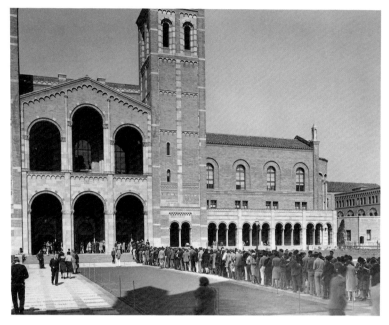

Registration line snaking across the Quad in the early thirties.

Royce Hall stage was often pressed into service as location for Registration and Enrollment in classes the thirties.

No publication about Royce Hall would be complete without the now famous snow scene of January 15, 1932. Several hours later, after students, faculty and staff arrived on campus, the white carpet was soon trampled into slush by hundreds of snowball fights.

A view of the original seating during installation. The chandeliers which can be seen at the edges of the picture were removed when the projection booth was relocated in the early fifties. New chandeliers were designed and installed in the recent renovation.

This early thirties audience was taken, apparently, during an all Women's Hi Jinx program of which there were many in those pre-women's liberation days.

The original asbestos curtain being decorated. Its design was intended to replicate a medieval tapestry. The curtain was replaced shortly after World War II and its rigging was updated to meet curtain fire safety codes.

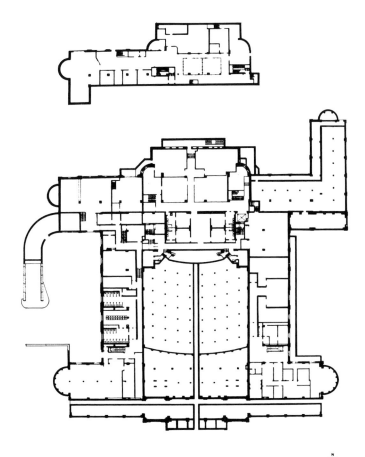

Floor plan of the basement and sub-basement.

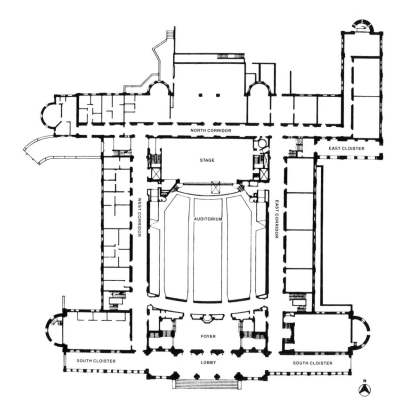

First floor plan view as it was prior to the remodeling.

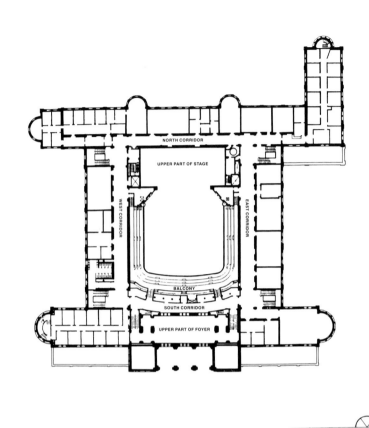

Second floor plan view prior to remodeling.

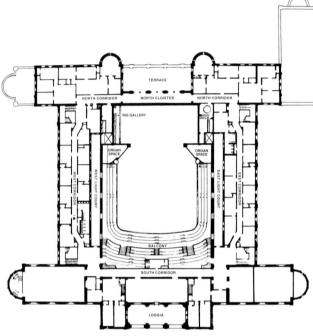

Third floor plan view.

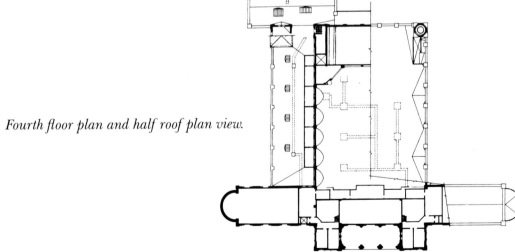

Fourth floor plan and half roof plan view.

ure to appear in Royce was John Dewey, the father of progressive education and one of the mentors of Ernest Carroll Moore; Dewey gave the principal address at the dedication of the new Westwood campus in 1930. Another former associate of Moore's, Jane Addams of Chicago's Hull House, spoke in the auditorium early in 1931.

Albert Einstein gave a major address to the student body in 1932, drawing a full auditorium. He spoke in German. His appearance was particularly significant as he was the only living person to be honored in the ceiling murals of Royce's first and third floor loggia.

Einstein and Jane Addams are among a long list of Nobel Laureates who have graced the stage of Royce; others include English poet T.S. Eliot, chemist Linus Pauling, philosopher Bertrand Russell, and United Nations Undersecretary Ralph Bunche. Bertrand Russell appeared during the controversial year he spent at UCLA as visiting professor, controversial because some members of the community objected to his unconventional social views and personal lifestyle. Pauling participated in a well-known debate with physicist Edward Teller on the merits of nuclear testing in the atmosphere, and he made numerous other appearances in the auditorium. Ralph Bunche, a UCLA graduate, talked to students about his experiences as a U.N. moderator in the Congo crisis.

Another famous speaker who discussed her work with the U.N. was Eleanor Roosevelt. Her 1950 program included selections by the Roger Wagner Chorale and an introduction by Provost Clarence Dykstra.

Albert Einstein spoke in Royce Hall on February 15, 1932, while on an extended visit to Southern California to participate in a series of seminars at Caltech. He is shown here with Provost Moore mingling with students.

Bertrand Russell addresses a class during his visiting lectureship at UCLA. He had offices in Royce Hall and on many occasions the press would wander the halls of Royce looking for Russell's office in order to obtain his unique opinions on controversial issues.

George (at the piano) and brother Ira Gershwin gave their song "Strike Up the Band" to UCLA. Formal gift and acceptance ceremonies took place on Royce Hall stage during a student variety show.

Eleanor Roosevelt with Provost Clarence Dykstra immediately after her address in Royce Hall on January 19, 1950.

Arnold Schoenberg lectures to one of his many UCLA classes. He appeared many times in Royce Hall as part of numerous concerts which featured his compositions. For the eight years between his retirement and his death, he continued to compose and teach, privately, many UCLA graduate students in his nearby Pacific Palisades residence. Later, in 1956, the campus music building was named in his honor.

Julian Huxley, the English biologist, spoke in 1932, and his novelist brother, Aldous, followed him in 1943 in the first of a number of appearances. On the stage of Royce not long before his death in 1937, George Gershwin donated his *Strike Up the Band* to UCLA as a school song.

Historian Will Durant presented a series of lectures as early as 1935 and gave occasional talks in subsequent years. Fabian political scientist Harold Laski spoke in 1939, and another famous socialist, the revolutionary Russian premier Alexander Kerensky, talked to a student audience in 1959. English historian Arnold Toynbee addressed the campus community in 1963.

Such famous theologians or ministers as Martin Buber, Paul Tillich, Billy Graham, James Francis Cardinal McIntyre and James Pike have appeared before Royce audiences.

A number of outstanding creative figures have discussed their works and the creative process in general. Perhaps the earliest was Arnold Schoenberg, the atonal innovator who taught composition at UCLA in the 1940s. He delivered the annual Faculty Research Lecture: "The Composition with Twelve Tones" in 1941. In the same year dancer Katherine Dunham gave a popular lecture and demonstration to an afternoon audience of 800. In 1960 designer Buckminster Fuller gave a now-famous "marathon" lecture which held the attention of the audience from 8 p.m. to nearly 1 a.m., when it was discontinued to allow students some sleep before their 8 a.m. classes.

Political figures have not been strangers to Royce Hall, though they have often appeared on other than political missions. Jan Masaryk, the ill-fated Czechoslovakian foreign minister, was UCLA's Charter Day speaker in 1939, French statesman Pierre Mendes-France gave a talk in 1961, and Vice President Hubert Humphrey spoke at Charter Day in 1965. By that date, Charter Day exercises had outgrown Royce Hall, and Humphrey had been scheduled to speak outdoors, but rain forced a change in plans. The limited seating of Royce robbed the hall of many later famous figures who spoke elsewhere on campus: Lyndon Johnson, Dwight Eisenhower, Britain's Prince Phillip, Haile Selassie, and the Shah of Iran. President Harry Truman, however, lectured from Royce's stage in 1959, long after his term of office, drawing an appreciative audience. Gerald Ford, also speaking after his Presidential term had expired, addressed a Royce Hall crowd in 1978.

In UCLA's earlier days, political candidates were not allowed to make campaign speeches on campus—Estes Kefauver, for example, spoke from a truck parked at the curb on Hilgard Avenue—but when that regulation was relaxed, several famous names were added to the Royce Hall roster. John F. Kennedy, campaigning for the Presidency in 1959, arrived dramatically on the campus in a helicopter, walking up the hill to Royce and striding down the aisle of a full house to the stage. A few years later it was Richard Nixon, at the time a candidate for the governorship of California.

President Ronald Reagan's Royce Hall appearance was in his much earlier role as Hollywood movie star; he participated in the 1941 Homecoming Show with such other luminaries as his first wife Jane Wyman, Phil Silvers, Jimmy Durante, Joe E. Brown, Ann Rutherford, Alan Hale, Brenda Joyce and Dan Dailey, Jr.

Royce Hall has also been the site of a large number of conferences and symposia of the academic, scientific, and industrial world, ranging from such erudite subjects as numerical analysis to the down-to-

Harry Truman's ebullient remarks were preceded by his struggle, accompanied by Chancellor Raymond Allen, through a crowded hallway outside the stage door. He grumbled that his schedule got him up so early that he didn't have an opportunity to take care of personal obligations.

earth quarterly business forecasts. In the years when space travel was merely theoretical, the meetings of the Institute of Navigation brought together experts on celestial pathfinding in anticipation of guiding flights away from the earth.

During the period 1958–60, University Extension produced a burst of creative programming in the physical and social sciences which had a major impact on the community. In 1958, shortly after the launching of the first Russian Sputniks, Extension presented a course of 17 Monday evenings on space technology, attracting over 1,800 engineers and others to the auditorium. Among the stars of the series' roster were Werner Von Braun, James Van Allen, William Pickering and Simon Ramo.

In 1959–60, Extension broke new ground with a series of lectures on philosophy by famed UCLA philosopher Abraham Kaplan. Royce's capacity of 1,892 was oversubscribed, a rarity for such intellectual subject matter. Later in 1960 another large audience heard a series on Physics Today, delivered by the "father" of the H-bomb, Edward Teller. And, at the end of the year, British novelists C. P. Snow and Aldous Huxley, together with Huxley's wife Pamela Johnson and Nobel Laureate Harold Urey, presented a two-night seminar which was also oversubscribed.

In 1965, scientists from 73 nations gathered in Royce to discuss the results of the International Geophysical Year, a worldwide cooperative effort which studied many vital aspects of the earth. Other academic meetings and conferences have covered such topics as film, cryogenics, water ecology, metrics, low temperature physics, humanistic psychology, titanium, computing, and psychiatry in medicine.

John Kennedy is shown during his exciting appearance on Royce Hall stage on November 2, 1959, after he had declared his intention to run for the Presidency. After a short prepared address, Kennedy astounded the student audience with his quickness of response and facile wit in answering questions.

Overleaf: A picture of one of the many occasions when Royce Hall was too small to accommodate the anticipated crowd and the Quad in front of Royce was used as a program venue. Important events often seemed to take place either in Royce Hall or with Royce as an effective background. Provost Clarence Dykstra is shown addressing a student convocation during a post-World War II meeting in front of Royce.

THE PERFORMING ARTS SHARE THE STAGE

The role of Royce Hall as a leading center for the performing arts is an outstanding fulfillment of Provost Moore's prediction of a future "greater than any of us can foresee." Certainly Moore did not imagine the future importance of Royce Hall as a cultural asset of the community, with frequent appearances by world-famed public figures. Quite the contrary; in Moore's own words, "Almost the first outsider who came to do business with us was an amusement broker who asked, 'What names will you have for your artist series?' We told him we were not going to have 'an artist series'; that Gibbon wrote of the Romans that in all matters of art the Greeks were the performers, the Romans merely the spectators, and that our people would make their own music and not employ others merely to get amusement from them."

True to this principle, the first performances in Royce were mostly student events: frequent productions of the University Dramatics Society and the irreverent student revues called Campus Capers, and later the All-U Sings and Homecoming Shows, which included participants from the motion picture world, including one who later became President of the United States. One series with serious cultural ambitions was the annual Greek Drama coached by Classics instructor Evalyn Thomas, who somehow managed to get UCLA athletes and student leaders into Grecian tunics to portray the tragic heroes of Aeschylus and Euripides.

Among the earliest traditional performances in Royce, however, was one with a strong professional aspect: the tri-weekly organ concerts by University Organist Alexander Schreiner and a host of equally noted guest performers. No doubt Provost Moore considered Schreiner one of "our people," since he was on the staff of the University, though he was not only a professional organist but an outstanding one, and the instrument on which he performed was exceptional.

Alexander Schreiner, UCLA's first University Organist, at the console of the four manual Skinner pipe organ. The Royce Hall organ played an important role in the cultural life of many generations of UCLA students.

One of the annual Greek dramas during the thirties. Production of these plays influenced the allocation of space in Royce for an adequate stage house and rigging system. Otherwise, Royce might have been finished as an assembly hall with inadequate staging facilities.

A typical recital scene in Royce Hall.

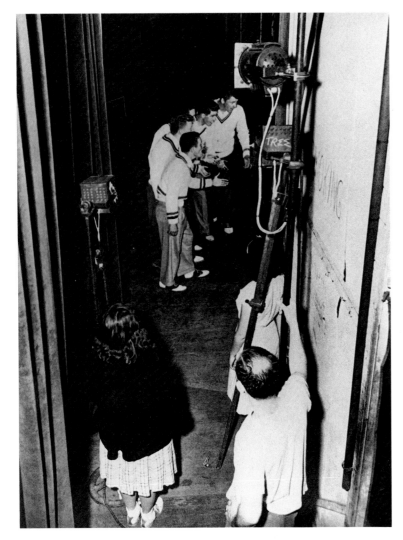

A backstage photograph taken during an All-U Sing, the popular thirties-forties-fifties student talent programs that often featured personalities from the motion picture studios.

Famed performer, Carol Burnett, '54, in a scene from a student written and directed musical comedy, Love Thy Coach. Produced on Royce Hall stage in May 1954, it featured Burnett, then a student, in the starring role of a female coach on a small college football team which achieves national ranking under her guidance.

One of Moore's fondest dreams for Royce Hall was that it should be equipped with a fine pipe organ, and a generous gift from the Harvey Mudd family made that possible. To design and install the instrument, Moore enlisted the services of Harold Gleason, a well-known organist and founder of the department of organ at the Eastman School of Music, Rochester, New York. Gleason visited Royce Hall and made a number of trips to supervise the year-long construction of the organ at the Massachusetts factory of the Skinner Organ Company. He judged the side chambers provided for the organ in Royce to be unsuited to the big instrument, and he persuaded the architects to allow the pipes to be placed over the proscenium arch.

After spending three months in the summer of 1930 installing and tuning the organ, Gleason was invited to give the inaugural concert on September 9. He selected a program of works which would best demonstrate the powers and quality of the new instrument. Among the selections was a piece composed for the occasion by Josiah Royce's son, Edward, a faculty member of the Eastman School's composition department. Royce chose as his theme the story of Everyman, a favorite of his father's.

Evaluating the organ, one critic wrote, "The build-up is stunning, and it struck me that in all grades of dynamics there was a transparency unusual in organs of this size. . . . The installation of this splendid instrument is a great thing for Southern California, and it should be tremendously good in creating a taste for real organ music."

Alexander Schreiner, who was later to become organist of the Mormon Tabernacle in Salt Lake

A view of the organ pipes over the proscenium arch.

The organ console. Mrs. Seeley Mudd, mother of Harvey Mudd, was the donor of the organ. The Mudd family, noted Southern California philanthropists, originally intended to fund a student union building. The family has funded many valuable educational facilities and programs in colleges and universities throughout Southern California.

Professor and University Organist Thomas Harmon at the console of the Royce Hall organ.

City, inaugurated a series of Tuesday, Friday and Sunday recitals which became famous not only on campus but in the community. Many years afterwards, in 1969, another inaugural concert was given on the organ, to mark the conclusion of a major renovation of the instrument supervised by the current University Organist, Thomas Harmon. This time the recitalist was Schreiner. The Gleason family figured in another event when Gleason's wife, Catharine Crozier, played the fiftieth anniversary concert in 1980. On that occasion, she duplicated the inaugural program of 1930 with the exception of two works for which the music was not available.

The strictly home-talent concept of Provost Moore was not to prevail. The programming of off-campus professionals began in earnest in 1935–36 with four concerts by the Los Angeles Philharmonic conducted by Otto Klemperer. The campus yearbook described these events as "the first time that a symphony orchestra has ever performed at any college," a statement long on enthusiasm and possibly short on accuracy.

In 1936 Moore resigned, and the campus was administered for a year by University of California President Robert Gordon Sproul, who appointed a Committee on Drama, Lectures and Music (the predecessor of today's Committee on Fine Arts Productions). The committee was to present "a musical event each year," and its first effort brought the Vienna Choir Boys to UCLA on February 4, 1937. The performing arts program centered in Royce Hall was thus established, and over the decades the yearly menu of offerings has continued to grow.

At first these cultural events were designed ex-

The earliest prestige cultural program on Royce Hall stage was the presentation of the Los Angeles Philharmonic conducted by Otto Klemperer. The above picture shows the orchestra with chorus in a performance of Beethoven's Ninth Symphony. Klemperer is at the center of the stage. The Los Angeles Philharmonic has, from the early thirties, been a constant performer at Royce Hall. Its remarkable recordings with Zubin Mehta were all recorded in Royce.

One of the wide variety of cultural events which Royce Hall stage has served. Royce became famous for its chamber orchestra performances.

clusively to serve the campus community of faculty, staff and students. Season tickets were sold primarily on campus in 1937 for the first subscription series, which included Marian Anderson, John Charles Thomas, the Budapest String Quartet and the Los Angeles Philharmonic. The third season (Nino Martini, Angna Enters, Bartlett and Robertson, Bidu Sayao, Raya Garbousova and Donald Dickson, and the Devi Dja Balinese Dancers) did not sell enough season tickets to sustain the program. Student organizations were asked to help sell season tickets, and many, such as Spurs, a campus women's service group, worked hard on the campaign. The series was saved from early extinction, and the fourth series (Yehudi Menuhin, Igor Gorin, Helen Jepson, La Argentinita and Artur Rubinstein) was a success. The student yearbook pronounced the concerts "one of *the* campus social events." However, it soon became apparent that it was not practical to limit the cultural program to a campus audience. Gradually, more and more of the general public, particularly those who lived close to UCLA, became regular patrons of the Royce Hall events, and eventually they were the majority of ticket buyers.

As the programming grew, Royce became something more than a college auditorium; it began to fill the role of a second cultural center in Los Angeles, serving especially the western part of the city. Moreover, it did not merely duplicate downtown programming on a smaller scale; it began to offer many events which were uniquely its own. For example, the Los Angeles Music Festival under the direction of its founder, Franz Waxman, moved from its original home in Beverly Hills and presented its annual series in Royce each May and June. Waxman, a composer and conductor, was able to attract not only an

Artur Rubinstein gave a record number of eight recitals in Royce Hall. Additionally, two of his children attended UCLA. John, his son, was prominent in Musical Theater Workshop and sang and acted many times on Royce Hall stage.

Franz Waxman's Los Angeles Music Festival was the magnet which brought many world-class performing artists to Royce Hall. He was a prominent motion picture music composer, arranger, and conductor who received many Oscar nominations and several Oscar awards. Many of his arrangements are in the repertory of major symphony orchestras throughout the world.

orchestra of quality but artists of world repute, and the Festival found a congenial home in Royce Hall for over 20 years.

The Festival was soon joined by another unique series produced by the Los Angeles Chamber Symphony Orchestra founded by Harold Byrns and led by such guest conductors as Igor Stravinsky, Izler Solomon and Maurice Abravenal. After a hiatus of some years, the orchestra was revived under the direction of Gerard Swartz and again offered its series in Royce Hall.

Another group, which appeared in Royce for over 25 years, was an orchestra conducted by Henri Temianka, the organizer and principal violinist of the Paganini String Quartet. His ensemble presented a series of Sunday evening concerts conducted under the title of "Let's Talk Music" and later as the California Chamber Symphony. For a number of years Temianka also presented the Saturday afternoon Concerts for Youth.

Two outstanding training orchestras for young instrumentalists have also performed regularly in Royce Hall. One, conducted by Mehli Mehta, founder of the Bombay Symphony, is the American Youth Symphony, which each year presents the public with free concerts of major symphonic works. The other is the Debut Orchestra of the Young Musicians Foundation. Among the alumni of its conductors' training are such established maestros as Lawrence Foster, Michael Tilson Thomas and Myung Wha Chung.

Dance has constituted an important item on the Royce Hall cultural menu from the start. Trudi Schoop and her company appeared on the artists series as early as 1939, and the roll of subsequent performers contains the names of nearly every important troupe, from the American Ballet Theatre and Martha Graham to the Ballet Russe, the Bejart Ballet, Robert Joffrey, Twyla Tharp and Bella Lewitzky.

Student dance entered the scene as early as the mid-thirties with the annual Dance Recital under the leadership of Professor Martha Deane of Women's Physical Education. The recital soon became a principal event of the academic year, attracting student workers from art and music as well. Even after professional companies were brought into the picture by the Committee on Drama, Lectures and Music, the recital continued to be part of the series, changing its name to Dance Concert. In later years, the Department of Dance has worked closely with Fine Arts Productions to ensure a professional series which is an academic adjunct to the curriculum, involving visiting companies in residencies and master classes as well as the usual public performances.

Dance Recital production of Fledermaus, *May 1941. The Dance Recital was a true amalgam of students and staff from Drama, Art, Music, Physical Education and other majors from as far afield as Physics and English. There was no Dance major or Department of Dance at that time. The Dance Recital was a true all-university effort.*

The Bella Lewitzky Dance Company is shown during the final Royce Hall performance before the closing for renovation on February 12, 1983. Lewitsky performed in many programs as a young dancer with the Lester Horton Dance Company and later returned, even more frequently, to Royce Hall with her own company. She is shown here addressing the company during the pre-performance warm-up exercises.

Igor Stravinsky is shown about to conduct the Los Angeles Chamber Orchestra. This picture was taken prior to one of the many concerts which Stravinsky conducted in Royce. A "neighbor" of UCLA for many years, he performed not only his orchestral works in Royce but also served as pit conductor of two fully staged productions of two of his operas, L'Histoire du Soldat and Mavra.

His production of L'Histoire du Soldat, in 1949 as a part of the Los Angeles Music Festival, was outstanding for its combination of stellar talent: Henry Schnitzler, son of the famed Viennese author Arthur Schnitzler and then a professor of theater arts at UCLA, was the stage director; Trudi Schoop, famed for her international dance company of comedic dancers, was the choreographer; Harry Horner, many times an Oscar and Tony winner for stage and motion picture design, was the designer; John Hoyt, prominent European and American stage and concert and film performer, played the Devil; Eduoard Franz, well-known stage and film actor, was the Narrator; and Antoinette Cobos, a French modern dancer imported from Paris by Stravinsky for this production, played the Dancer.

Igor Stravinsky is shown shaking hands with fellow conductor Alfred Wallenstein while Conrad Lester, prominent supporter of the arts in the Los Angeles community, and Dr. John Vincent (on right) UCLA professor of music and composer, look on. A number of Vincent's compositions were played by various orchestras in Royce Hall.

Jerome Hines started his singing career as a UCLA student in Chemistry in the early forties. He was an early winner of the Young Artists' Contest while singing in many campus concerts. After leaving UCLA, Hines went on to become one of the world's great bassos and a mainstay of the Metropolitan Opera Company. He has returned many times to give recitals in Royce Hall.

Drama, both foreign and domestic, is at home in Royce Hall, and among the famous actors to appear on its boards are Charles Laughton, Sir John Gielgud, Emlyn Williams, Charlton Heston, Marilyn Monroe, Burt Lancaster, Dame May Whitty, and Cornelia Otis Skinner.

The earliest dramas in Royce, however, were plays produced in the 1930s by the University Dramatics Society and supervised by a young actor/ director from the Pasadena Playhouse, Ralph Freud. After a few seasons, Freud attained academic status and was later instrumental in the founding of the Theater Arts Department. Until the department acquired its own building, most play preparation, including set construction, rehearsal and performance, took place in Royce.

Productions in foreign languages have been offered not only by the various UCLA language departments but by such well-known companies as the Tréteau de Paris and Die Schauspieltruppe Zurich. Operas have ranged from such standard works as *La Traviata* and *Faust* to such rarities as *Jenufa* and *The Sinking of the Titanic*.

Films, especially in the early years before the Theater Arts Department had its own facilities, were a frequent part of Royce's programming, particularly of such classics as *Nanook of the North, Intolerance, Children of Paradise, The Gold Rush, Grand Illusion* and *The Great Train Robbery*.

As the cultural programming of the hall continued to expand, it became apparent that there was a need in the community to provide something more than the standard cultural menu. The programming committee took on the responsibility of adding new, avant-garde forms of expression and events of interest to special groups. Many of these presentations were fortunate to break even at the box office, but the University felt it necessary to offer them a platform. In the absence of such availability, their artists would likely never receive the public exposure so necessary for creative work to flourish.

The annual Young Artists Contest and Concert was an early forerunner of later adventures such as the Twentieth Century Music series, ethnomusic and dance progamming, the modern dance series, and early career concerts for domestic and foreign artists testing their acceptance by U.S. audiences. A number of the latter who were to become internationally renowned artists made early appearances on Royce's stage. For example, Luciano Pavarotti's second engagement in the United States was in Royce Hall.

In addition to the members of faculty-administration committees which have guided the cultural program, its operation has required a professional staff nearly from the beginning. The first executive head was Frances Inglis, who built a national and international reputation for the program; both for its size and sophistication. One noted critic characterized Royce Hall as one of the two most prominent performance platforms in the Western United States.

Ms. Inglis' successor, after 1973, was Edmond Harris, who increased the number of offerings and encouraged new and avant-garde performers. In 1979 he was followed by Pebbles Wadsworth, who not only attracted additional international events but steered the program through the difficult period during the Royce renovation when other halls had to be used.

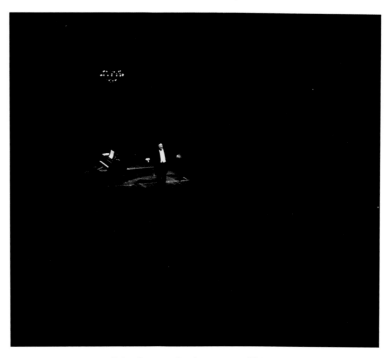

Luciano Pavarotti is shown during one of his recitals in Royce Hall.

THE SOUND OF ROYCE ON RECORD

The art of concert hall acoustics was still in its infancy when Royce Hall was designed. Practitioners of the art were still not in full agreement as to why rooms such as the Grossemusikvereinsaal in Vienna, Leipzig's Gewandhaus or Boston's Symphony Hall were such great projectors of music while other halls, often designed much later, were inadequate or unsatisfactory.

UCLA was fortunate to have on its faculty Professor Vern O. Knudsen, an acoustical physicist in the forefront of research in the field. He was asked to work on the acoustical design of the Royce Hall auditorium, and he devoted much time to the assignment. He prescribed textures and finishes for the room to produce the best sound possible within the technology of the time. The walls were surfaced with acoustical plaster containing small openings as deep as three-quarters to one inch from the surface, and the original color was "pounced" on the surface to assure that no paint treatment would seal off the acoustic properties of the plaster.

As the years passed and the science of room acoustics developed—much of it in Knudsen's own laboratory—Knudsen kept a consistent and watchful ear on Royce Hall. From time to time he made tests in the auditorium which led to recommendations for corrective installations. This striving for acoustical perfection was an important consideration when plans for the recent renovation were being prepared.

The acoustical properties of Royce were well known to the recording industry, and in time the auditorium became the site of a number of classical and popular recording sessions. The earliest of these

The setting for the Los Angeles Philharmonic recordings. The London Decca engineers inspected and tested many suggested recording sites in Los Angeles before deciding on Royce Hall as the ideal location for this prestigious series of albums. They directed the construction of a stage extension over forty feet into the auditorium. The installation often had to be set in and taken out overnight to accommodate the regular public performance schedule. Special lighting had to be provided because of the stage extension into the seating areas. Recording engineers insisted on the placement of the orchestra "out into the hall" to take advantage of Royce Hall's remarkable acoustics—now permanently preserved in many fine recordings.

(in 1954) produced a "Starlight Concert" with the Hollywood Bowl Symphony Orchestra (the Los Angeles Philharmonic) under the direction of Carmen Dragon.

An important series of recordings began in 1967 when London Decca chose Royce Hall for a recording of the Los Angeles Philharmonic under the baton of Zubin Mehta. To make this session possible, the British company flew more than two and a half tons of recording equipment over the Pole from London to Los Angeles. Although the recording crew had to work around Royce Hall performances

by the American Ballet Theatre and an evening lecture, the resulting album was described as one with "spectacular sound." As a consequence, the Decca recording sessions continued on an annual basis until the end of Mehta's service with the orchestra.

The lively sound of Royce has also been heard in several motion pictures, including the organ music in the christening scene in *The Godfather*, and some of the choral background music from *Tron*. Among popular music albums recorded there are one by Howard Rumsey and the Lighthouse All Stars called *Jazz Rolls Royce* and another by Frank Zappa.

A recording session in progress. The musicians are often at optimum performance level in the relaxed, informal environment of recording sessions sans formal attire and the heat and glare of performance spotlights.

Zubin Mehta is shown conducting the Philharmonic in a recording session. The musicians are positioned around him for quadraphonic recordings.

Reviewing the tapes in the control room: Danny Kaye (with hat) had been narrator for one of the records just completed. The vast amount of equipment shown in the room was flown each year from London (56 cases in all) and set up in Royce Hall for the recordings.

Reviewing the tapes in the control room: Zubin Mehta is shown in the center, Ray Minshull (London Decca record producer) on the right, and David Frisina, concert-master, on the left gesturing to Mehta.

THE MEMORABLE AND THE BIZARRE

Royce Hall has survived a number of near-disasters and witnessed a good many events which were either stirring, unusual or comical. The building has come through two sizable earthquakes without serious injury and escaped major damage from three fires and a flood.

The first of the quakes was the Long Beach temblor of 1933; it occurred on the Inglewood fault, one branch of which extends up to the campus. Royce Hall weathered the shaking with little more than some paint flaking from the decorated ceiling. In the major Sylmar quake of 1971, the principal damage was the knocking over of pipes in the organ loft.

Royce Hall's flood, in 1980, arose from a peculiar source—a gate crasher trying to get into a Cannonball Adderly Tribute which had attracted 800 people to the auditorium. The crasher tried to enter Royce through a smoke vent in the roof, but his weight snapped off a sprinkler head on a fire line, releasing 165 pounds of water pressure. A gentle rain fell on the stage, soaking scenery, draperies and the electronic gear in the orchestra. The break in the fire line alerted the local fire department, bringing trucks with red lights flashing and sirens screaming into the quadrangle and disgorging firemen who streamed down the aisles, effectively putting a stop to the concert. Before the source of the shower could be discovered, four inches of water had flooded the dressing rooms and the organ blower room and poured into a cable containing 2,600 pairs of telephone lines. The resulting short circuit caused a small fire in the General Telephone service build-

A photo of organ pipe damage from the 1971 Sylmar earthquake. The center of gravity of the larger metal pipes was so high that the swaying knocked them over onto the smaller ranks in the front.

ing in Westwood and shut down telephone service to the UCLA hospital for over six hours.

Royce Hall's first stage fire occurred in 1930 as the curtain was about to rise on that year's edition of the student Campus Capers. A photographer taking a backstage picture of the Men's Glee Club set off a large burst of flashpowder, igniting the back of the velvet curtain. Stagehands lowered the big asbestos curtain, grabbed fire extinguishers, doused the flames, and cleaned up the resulting carbon-colored mess on the stage. Members of the Glee Club, nattily clad in blue blazers and white flannels, went into their act in the best show-must-go-on tradition, not realizing that the soaked curtain would drip on the stage floor, forming a considerable puddle. Nothing daunted, the Glee Club went through its full routine, including rolling on the floor, and ended up looking much like coal miners after a full day's work.

The second fire, in 1941, disrupted a student performance of *Green Grow the Lilacs* (later to become the musical favorite, *Oklahoma*). Actors were to carry flaming torches on stage on their way to the climactic haystack fire, and the prop man had prepared tin cups on sticks to hold small balls of alcohol-soaked cotton. As the actors entered the stage, however, some of the flaming balls spilled onto the floor. The actors panicked and began to roll their bodies over the burning cotton, but the alcohol then began to burn their costumes. At that juncture, the stage manager walked out with a fire extinguisher and, in full view of the audience, proceeded to quench not only the increasing conflagration but the serious mood of the drama as well.

A more threatening fire broke out in 1949 as the stage crew was preparing for a performance by Spanish dancer Carmelita Maracci. A crew member inadvertently turned on a lighting circuit which ignited scenery stacked against the rear wall, and in a matter of minutes the wall was a single sheet of flame. The crew called the fire department and attacked the blaze with backstage hoses, putting out the fire before the engines arrived. As it was only 7 p.m., there was time to clean up the debris before admitting the audience to another gala Royce Hall performance.

Significant political occasions in Royce go back at least to September 1938, when 1,500 students gathered in the hall to hear a live radio broadcast by Adolf Hitler as he prepared to consolidate his position in central Europe, ending his talk with an ominous, "I have been a front line soldier, and I know what war is." A little over three years later, on December 8, 1941, the auditorium was filled by students still in shock over the incredible news of Pearl Harbor the previous day. They heard the live broadcast of President Roosevelt's famed "day of infamy" address to the House and Senate as war was declared.

A Homecoming "Liberty" show about 1944 takes some unusual curtain calls. The ticket sales from such productions helped the sale of war bonds.

Students took an even more active campus role in the events surrounding the war in Vietnam, and they were the sometimes vocal participants in a dramatic Academic Senate meeting called in Royce in May 1970, to discuss the possibility of closing the University following the Kent State shootings. In spite of mass tension among the student spectators, the meeting reached an orderly conclusion, and the University completed its spring term.

One of the more unusual events of the term

Zubin Mehta conducting The Messiah *in front of Royce. The performance was organized by students and faculty of the Department of Music as a gesture of peace and community during the unrest of the period. Note the flag at half-mast in the background in memory of the Kent State shootings, which had a profound impact on all universities and colleges.*

was a quickly-organized outdoor performance of Handel's *Messiah* on the plaza in front of Royce Hall on May 18. The orchestra, led by famed conductor Zubin Mehta, was composed of players from the UCLA Symphony and the Los Angeles Philharmonic in concert with UCLA choral groups. The event was intended to offer support for the students' protests but to suggest that their aims be achieved in a peaceful way.

Many years earlier, another politically potent event failed to live up to official apprehension. Paul Robeson had been engaged to sing a Royce Hall concert shortly after he had returned from Russia openly critical of the American government. Professor Gustave Arlt, chairman of the Committee on Drama, Lectures and Music, learned that Robeson had interrupted two concerts elsewhere by delivering a controversial political address. Arlt warned the basso that if that happened at UCLA he would ring down the curtain. Sure enough, in the second half of the program, Robeson stopped after one of his numbers and prepared to speak. Glancing at Arlt in the wings, he devoted his magnificent speaking voice to—the Gettysburg Address.

An even more delicate situation developed during a 1967 lecture by George Lincoln Rockwell, a leader of the American Nazi movement. Most of those in the half-filled auditorium were strongly opposed to his views, and his talk was often interrupted by angry shouts. A bomb threat delivered backstage during the talk was discounted as a hoax, but protestors discovered his automobile parked at the stage door and let all the air out of the tires. Campus police were faced with the likelihood of a riot when Rockwell attempted to leave the auditorium. At the

Another view of Mehta conducting The Messiah.

Paul Robeson was once of the many great artists to perform in Royce Hall during the early years of the Great Artists' Series. Appearances such as his put the Series in the forefront of major performing arts programs.

Applause and cheering greet the finale of The Messiah. *Once again, Royce Hall served the campus community as a gathering place and focus of its activities and concerns.*

A close-up view of the scenic elements of HMS (Royce Hall) Titanic.

end of the lecture, he was quickly escorted off the stage, not to his tire-flattened car but to an exit from another building a safe distance away.

An outstanding symposium in the late '60s was colored by a bizarre incident. The event, sponsored by University Extension for the public, featured addresses by British novelists Aldous Huxley and C. P. Snow and Nobel Laureate Harold Urey. The auditorium staff, preparing to open the doors, found that someone had placed on each seat a flyer concerning the advent of someone calling himself Jesus Christ II. The staff hastily gathered up the tracts, but the program was barely under way when a man stood up near the stage, identified himself as Jesus Christ II and demanded to be heard. The program threatened to disintegrate when some members of the audience supported his right to speak. Before the proceedings eroded into chaos, the ushering staff and campus police removed him from the auditorium.

Not all of the unusual events in Royce were accidental; some were planned that way. An example was the 1966 opera, *The Bewitched*, by Harry Partch, a composer who had devised a complete orchestra of instruments of his own invention, including bowls that were stroked, objects struck with mallets, and stringed instruments of various shapes and sounds. The resulting work, while engaging, was markedly different from anything heard in the auditorium before or since.

A much later performance of a German opera, *The Sinking of the Titanic*, also qualified as a spectac-

The decoration of Royce Hall's towers simulates the smokestacks of the HMS Titanic for the opera The Sinking of the Titanic. *The platform in the middle of the Quad was set for the preliminary scenes of the launching of the ship, dedicatory speeches and music, and the introduction of various members of the ship's "company and crew."*

The stage setting for The Sinking of the Titanic *included a huge symbolic anchor chain. The organ loft over the proscenium arch served as the location of the "crow's nest" scene. The city of West Berlin sent over 400 performers and workers to Los Angeles to present the six-week-long cultural festival of which this opera was but one event.*

ular departure. This work, presented in 1981, was a birthday gift from the city of West Berlin to Los Angeles' 200th Anniversary celebration. The staging of the opera involved audience participation as passengers in the sinking of the ill-fated vessel, which was recreated in various parts of the building. The "passengers" entered Royce Hall to the music of the "ship's" band on the deck, were divided into "first class" and "steerage" sections, witnessed the gaiety and the subsequent panic in the "grand ballroom," and were eventually led (with women and children separated for rescue) through the sub-basement to survival or "drowning."

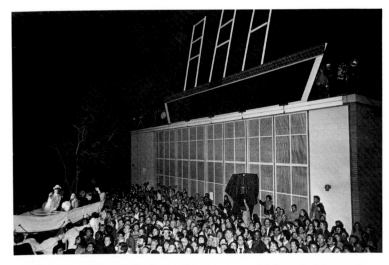

In the rear of Royce Hall the final scenes of The Sinking of the Titanic *were played on "abandon ship" platforms. The audiences were led from the auditorium, over the stage, and down two stories through the sub-basement and out onto the parking lot which simulated the Atlantic Ocean. As the ship sank, the "first class" passengers were saved, the "third class" passengers were drowned, and the "second class" passengers (the audience) were left to fend for themselves.*

A more conventional but nonetheless remarkable evening in Royce occurred in November 1958, when more than 1,500 persons joined in the celebration of Carl Sandburg's 80th birthday. Chaired by Shakespearean scholar Frank Baxter, the evening featured readings by such performers as Jeff Chandler and Martha Hyer and was climaxed by the appearance of the tousled white-haired celebrant himself, with ever-ready guitar in hand. Sandburg entertained the celebrity-studded audience with readings of his works and a number of his inimitable folk songs.

Whether avant-garde or conventional, the steady stream of cultural and academic programming in the auditorium has made Royce Hall a famous name. Its wide repute is in sharp contrast to the level of recognition revealed by an incident in 1936, a few years after the building's construction. Charter Day exercises that year honored Nobelist Alexis Carrel, but a news photographer dispatched by a local paper arrived a bit late and breathlessly asked bystanders, "Where is this guy—Royce? I've got to get a shot of him. Has he shown up yet?" The response: "Royce? He's been dead for 25 years. That's the name of this building. Carrel is the boy you want—he's already marched in."

Carl Sandburg's 80th birthday anniversary celebration provided the occasion for one of the many gala performances in Royce Hall. In the picture above Sandburg is shown receiving an award from Wilbur Smith, UCLA librarian, on the left and rare book collector Jake Zeitlin on the right.

Unusual photo taken in the early thirties.

THE NEW ROYCE INSIDE THE OLD

The 1983–84 renovations of Royce Hall were the most extensive ever undertaken, but there had been a number of others during the life of the structure. As mentioned earlier, Royce was originally the principal classroom building of the new campus, and as other classroom structures were erected, some of the rooms in Royce were converted to fill more pressing needs. One large lecture hall became the departmental and faculty office headquarters for Business Administration; another was rebuilt to serve as a little theater for the Department of Theater Arts. One of the greatest changes took place in the sub-basement at the rear of the building which had originally housed the campus heating plant.

When the first buildings were constructed in 1929, Royce Hall was close to the center of the campus, and it was a logical place to locate the huge boilers which would supply heat and hot water to all the structures. From the sub-basement steam and other utilities were routed to the rest of the campus; this system still exists, but the heat source was removed from Royce Hall in 1953 and relocated in a new and larger steam plant elsewhere. The sub-basement was then converted for use as shops and storage.

Another change, though a minor one, took place in Royce's towers. The east tower of Royce was the original home of the UCLA chimes, capable of striking the hour in melodious tones or of producing musical selections from a keyboard located in a room under Royce's balcony. The chimes were a gift of Count and Mrs. Frederic Thorne-Rider of Bel-Air, where the sound of the chimes usually reached. Most

listeners envisioned a large rack of bells in the tower; actually there were four loudspeakers which broadcast the amplified sound. During World War II, the loudspeakers became part of the campus air raid warning system—a service that was never needed. After the war, the chimes were moved. The speakers were placed in the tower of Powell Library, and the playing console was relocated to a room in the basement of Schoenberg Hall.

Until the recent remodeling, few changes had been made in the auditorium itself except for painting and refurbishing and minor structural alterations in the interest of earthquake safety. By the late 1970s it had become apparent that the auditorium needed to be upgraded to meet the standards established by newer performance centers in Los Angeles. The years had given Royce a patina which only age can grant, but many of the physical characteristics were far out of date.

The floor of the auditorium was too flat to provide sight lines for the superb dance programs for which Royce had become famous. The rows of seats were too close for the comfort of a population which had grown larger with succeeding generations. The sound reinforcement system was 30 years out of date. The auditorium lighting, designed for student assemblies, was no longer sufficient for major performances. Building and fire codes had been changed over the years to require grounded electrical circuits, handicapped access to each floor and room, and pressurized fire sprinkler systems, among dozens of other required changes.

Lobbies, toilet facilities, ticket booths, dressing rooms, equipment storage rooms, the stage floor, room acoustics, the lighting control system, and even the truck access to deliver scenery, props and pianos to the stage—all needed critical study and evaluation for replacement or renovation.

A building committee was appointed, with broad representation of staff, students and faculty, and all users of the building were asked to submit lists of desirable improvements. Studies were conducted to determine traffic patterns, academic programming, community needs, room acoustics, and even weather conditions to verify the need to install air conditioning. The resulting data evolved into a prioritized list of design criteria for a major renovation project. A supervising architect was selected, the firm of John Carl Warnecke and Associates. Under the leadership of Charles Warner Oakley serving as the Warnecke project architect, a large and eminent professional staff of consultants was organized to provide the necessary expertise to solve the problems of mechanical improvements, art restoration, sound reinforcement, and dozens of other important engineering and aesthetic details. The critical task of acoustical design throughout the project was entrusted to acoustical consultants Ted Schultz and Ron McKay of Bolt, Beranek and Newman, Inc.

The task of remodeling an old building can be a more difficult and complex one than creating a totally new structure, for all planning has to respect the limits of the existing building. Major footings dictated some engineering decisions; available attic space between floors prescribed others. The square footage of the auditorium determined the number of seats which could be installed, the distance between the first floor and the balcony's reinforced concrete cantilevers dictated the height to which the orches-

tra-level floor could be tilted to provide better sight lines. The necessity for maintaining critical utilities services meant that the utilities tunnel directly beneath the orchestra pit had to remain, and the tunnel, in turn, prescribed the design of the orchestra pit elevator. And so it went through a long list of construction needs: sprinkler systems, electrical services, air conditioning, elevators, stairwell remodeling, loading docks, acoustical wall treatments, and even the refurbishing of the decor.

The project had a particular delicacy which influenced all planning and construction. Royce Hall is a building whose detail and silhouette are internationally known. Thousands of students, faculty, performers, artists, greats and near-greats, and generations of the Southern California community had worked in, studied in, and enjoyed the full range of artistic response within its walls for over 50 years. Their expectations made the Royce Hall renovation a project of great sensitivity.

Several years of intense planning and design finally produced a renovation program which satisfied the various groups. The project included a much-needed rehearsal facility on the west side of the building. The major public areas of the building

On top of the auditorium scaffolding. An artist is shown repainting the ceiling detail.

Auditorium filled with scaffolding to accommodate the work on the ceiling. The ceiling redecoration phase took two and a half months of meticulous artistic labor. It was the longest and most tedious part of the remodeling.

Demolition in the auditorium at the start of remodeling.

Beginning of reconstruction: windows have been sealed, new balcony forms are in place, and the downstairs floor has been re-sloped.

were to be air-conditioned. The auditorium's seating areas were to be remodeled to provide better sight lines, more leg room, and new seats. Wall surfaces were to be redesigned to enhance the acoustics of the already fine concert hall environment. There would be a new motion picture projection booth, a new sound reinforcement system, a new organ mechanical/electronic control system, increased lobby and public lounge space, new rest room facilities for both the first and second floors, and new dressing room facilities. There would also be new service facilities: elevators, stairways, catwalks, and other code-required elements.

Outside the public performance areas the plans called for new academic office spaces, a new Humanities Conference Hall, a new studio hall, and a new experimental theatre for the performing arts departments of instruction. Facilities for academic programs in fine arts, humanities, and other areas demanding well-equipped meeting space would be significantly enhanced.

Schematics, working drawings, and bid documents were developed and approved and contracts were signed and recorded. The last concert, by the Bella Lewitzky Dance Company, passed into history. The theatre was cleared of all equipment and materials to make way for the contractor. And finally, on February 22, 1983, the renovation project officially got underway.

Demolition crews stripped away wall and floor surfaces. Walls were torn down. Stairways and access holes were jackhammered. And problems germane to any remodeling project began to surface. Electrical circuits were discovered which were not on exist-

Orchestra pit excavation preparatory to installing the new orchestra pit elevator.

Following excavation, the steel structure for the new Rehearsal Hall on the west side of Royce is in place.

ing blueprints. Pipelines were not in places where engineers expected them to be. There were anomalies in wall and ceiling and floor areas to beset the workmen. A critical dimension between two pillars was found to differ from construction documents by a matter of a few important inches, requiring immediate architectural or engineering changes—workmen were waiting to proceed. Some of the revealed mysteries were advantageous to the project, some were costly and time-consuming, and many were historically curious and interesting.

But all efforts of planners, designers, engineers, craftsmen, and laboring crews combined to make Royce Hall remodeling a labor of love and respect. The most often-heard comment by a new crew coming to work on the project for the first time was one of admiration and awe at this magnificent and unique building and the expressed determination that ". . . this will be a fabulous place when we are finished."

Preceding Page: The artistry of architect Charles Warner Oakley superbly melded the new Rehearsal Hall addition into the existing building with such skill and elegance that the west side of the building now became one of the most attractive faces of Royce.

Opposite: A closer view of the new Rehearsal Hall exterior showing the new loading facility on the left.

The new Rehearsal Hall. This was one of the highest priority items of the remodeling project. It will increase the efficient use of the stage and auditorium by 30 to 50 percent.

The classroom areas were also remodeled as part of the project. State-of-the-art seating, lighting, and other classroom furnishings were installed in the classrooms in Royce keeping in the forefront the importance of Royce Hall to the educational mission of UCLA.

The west lobby created out of first floor offices and opening out onto the new terrace which caps the Rehearsal Hall.

Opposite page: The new terrace created on top of the Rehearsal Hall and accessed from the new west lobby. It has already become one of the most popular and sought-after gathering places for prestigious campus activities.

Following page: Looking toward the new west lobby from the remodeled "checkerboard" lobby. The ticket office has been relocated and the stairs to the balcony have been removed to provide access to the west lobby.

Unique view of the northeast stairwell, one of the outstanding interior architectural features of Royce.

The stage end of the auditorium prior to demolition and remodeling.

The "house" end of the auditorium prior to demolition and remodeling.

Overleaf: The "new" Royce Hall after the remodeling: new chandeliers, panels covering the organ pipes, repainted and redecorated ceiling, re-sloped orchestra and balcony seating, remodeled proscenium arch area to upgrade the room acoustics, and a new symphony shell enclosure.

A FACILITY FOR THE FUTURE

Today Royce Hall no longer rises from the pastoral setting in which it initially stood. Indeed, only a walk through the quadrangle bordered by the first four buildings can recapture the original feeling of architectural unity. The scene of the twin towers overshadowing the empty rolling foothills is preserved only in photographs or in the memory of the early classes. The activities of the University—the teaching, the research, the artistic performances—expanded so rapidly that it was abundantly clear within less than a generation that the vision of the original architects was not bold, but modest.

By the early 1950s the south campus began to sprout buildings to house the medical center and the expanding science research units. By the late 1950s the once lonely buildings around the original quadrangle were joined by the Humanities Buildings (now Rolfe and Campbell) to the north, and by Murphy Hall, the Law School and Dodd Hall to the east beyond the canyon, now filled in to accommodate Schoenberg Hall and the School of Architecture. Many other buildings have been added in the past generation, and the campus, seen from a distance or from the air, resembles more and more the historical city with its kaleidoscope of shapes and styles, crowding in on Royce which, one could argue, is now more integrated into its surroundings—as are the medieval cathedrals—than when it was isolated in an empty pasture.

The proliferation of buildings has been the most visible effect of the growth of the University, but far more impressive is the academic recognition received by the University. In the brief period of 50-odd years since the move to the Westwood campus, UCLA has risen from relative obscurity to a prominent position among the great universities of the nation, thus joining the ranks of the historic institutions whose seals adorn the ceiling of the Royce Hall foyer.

At the time the Westwood site was chosen, there was an unobstructed view of the Pacific Ocean from the hills at the north end of the campus. A viewer, conscious of the end of the continent, might well feel that this university, like others on the West Coast, represented the westernmost reach of what was known as Western Civilization. Today, horizons are less provincial; Californians realize that they are on the eastern edge of the great Pacific Basin, rimmed with rich cultures to the west and the south with which there is much communication in politics, commerce and cultural exchange. The University no longer conceives itself as a frontier outpost but as a center of intellectual influence radiating in all directions. The jets that fly to New York or Rome fly as readily to Tokyo or Peking or Mexico City or Rio de Janeiro. The eclecticism embodied in the Romanesque style has enabled the University to grow with the needs of new circumstances and technologies.

Royce Hall has witnessed all these changes: the physical growth of the campus, the academic development of the University, the expansion of its horizons. Throughout, the majestic towers have represented continuity and stability. In time, however, Royce Hall itself had to adapt to the new scope of the University, an adaptation not in its external beauty but in its internal functions. After two generations of intensive use, the auditorium, the classrooms and the offices were sorely in need of

renovation and modernization to meet the current demands upon them. Through 1983–84's extensive renewal project, the entire building within a building was renovated.

Royce Hall has again become the focal point of a great many University activities. As the University reached international distinction, it was in keeping with the original vision of the architects that Royce Hall should undergo this major renovation, a renewal which has enhanced its serviceability without changing its imposing and reassuring presence.

The campus about 1930. Royce Hall is still a significant landmark in the surrounding area.

Opposite: The auditorium view of the "new" Royce Hall showing the revised projection booth/rear wall area, new balcony front design, new side wall treatment to provide better room acoustics, and new seating for audience comfort.

The campus about 1940. Dominated by Royce Hall, the campus has completed its first decade on the Westwood site and is about to enter the World War II period with planning started for post-war expansion.

UNIVERSITY OF CALIFORNIA
AT LOS ANGELES
DAVID C ALLISON - SUPERVISING ARCHITECT
RALPH D. CORNELL - LANDSCAPE ARCHITECT
MAY - 1945

Supervising Architect David Allison's master plan for post-World War II expansion and development. Compare this with the original George Kelham master plan of 1926 (page 15). The Allison Plan shows the "gully" filled in to provide expansion building sites and brings the planning map up to date.

*UCLA about 1950, before the great building boom which trans-
formed the southern end of the campus.*

A longer view of the almost but never quite completed Westwood and UCLA campus taken about 1970. UCLA's and Los Angeles' building boom has all but buried Royce Hall, once proudly dominant over empty fields, within a forest of architectural development.

The view from the blue hills to the sea.

MONTPELLIER

PARIS

BOLOGNA

LEYDEN

UPSALA

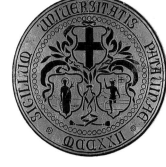

PADUA

PRAGUE

SALAMANCA

HEIDELBERG

OXFORD

CAMBRIDGE

European university seals located on the beams of the outer lobby.

ON STAGE

Auditorium Appearances

The transformation of Royce Hall from an auditorium for student assemblies into a recognized symbol of Western educational thought and a premier platform for the best in the performing arts did not occur overnight. It was achieved over a period of five decades by the academic growth of the campus on which it stands and by a never-ending procession of famous speakers, public figures and artists in every field. These world-class personages brought to the expanding campus community a continuing involvement with political, social, cultural and educational developments.

Academicians, politicians, philosophers, poets, musicians, dancers and performers of every kind have provided a stimulating fare, challenging Royce Hall audiences to think in new ways and to enjoy a kaleidoscopic variety of arts and culture. In return, Royce Hall offers performers an appreciative and sophisticated reception.

It would be impractical and probably tiresome to present a complete compendium of every public figure, academician and artist who has ever appeared in Royce, but a selected chronology of some of the more significant performers and productions of this remarkable facility provides considerable insight into the reason for the hall's influence on the wider community. Such a list follows.

The date indicates the time of appearance or "first" appearance.
*denotes more than one appearance.
†denotes Nobel Laureate.

Academicians

†Sir Norman Angell	*April 12, 1944*
Jacques Barzun	*August 7, 1959*
†George Wells Beadle	*March 27, 1962*
Laura Boulton	*May 21, 1947*
Martin Buber	*March 21, 1961*
†Alexis Carrel	*March 20, 1936*
Kenneth Bancroft Clark	*May 7, 1968*
†Arthur Compton	*March 27, 1930*
†F.H.C. Crick	*March 9, 1965*
John Dewey	*March 30, 1930*
Mrs. W.E.B. Dubois	*November 13, 1970*
Rene Dubos	*October 26, 1972*
Alfred Frankfurter	*March 23, 1961*
*Buckminster Fuller	*January 28, 1960*
William Ernest Hocking	*November 13, 1944*
Joel Hildebrand	*April 8, 1941*
E. Stanley Jones	*March 20, 1941*
Julian Huxley	*October 26, 1932*
*Abraham Kaplan	*November 11, 1957*
Barnaby Keeney	*February 16, 1966*
Clark Kerr	*September 26, 1958*
Rollo May	*March 6, 1959*
Margaret Mead	*March 29, 1960*
Raymond Moley	*January 16, 1931*
†Thomas Hunt Morgan	*February 28, 1930*
Hans Morgenthau	*November 20, 1965*
†Gunnar Myrdal	*May 4, 1966*
J. Robert Oppenheimer	*May 4, 1964*
Alfred Noyes	*October 30, 1940*
†*Linus Pauling	*March 18, 1958*
Jacques Piccard	*October 29, 1978*
†Carl Rogers	*April 3, 1967*
†Bertrand Russell	*March 31, 1939*
*Jonas Salk	*February 18, 1972*
Robert Scalapino	*November 20, 1965*
B. F. Skinner	*December 2, 1963*
Lyman Beecher Stowe	*January 9, 1931*
Harold Sverdrup	*March 23, 1938*
*Edward Teller	*October 6, 1960*
Paul Tillich	*March 25, 1963*
†Harold Urey	*December 18, 1960*
Barbara Ward	*April 3, 1957*
*Norbert Weiner	*May 27, 1949*
Gregory Zilborg	*October 20, 1947*

Authors

W. A. Auden	*March 17, 1954*
Charles Beard	*February 7, 1959*
Eric Bentley	*March 31, 1964*
Jacob Bronowski	*December 13, 1964*
John Mason Brown	*April 21, 1958*
Lewis Browne	*September 30, 1936*
Erwin D. Canham	*January 28, 1965*
*Bennett Cerf	*March 2, 1953*
John Ciardi	*April 17, 1964*
Henry Steele Commager	*April 7, 1976*
Marc Connelly	*May 23, 1941*
Norman Corwin	*June 1, 1961*
*Will Durant	*July 1, 1935*
†Thomas Stearns Eliot	*January 6, 1933*
John Erskine	*November 2, 1939*
*Lion Feuchtwanger	*October 1, 1943*
Douglas Southall Freeman	*March 25, 1947*
Hamlin Garland	*March 3, 1937*
Harry Golden	*December 13, 1964*
Paul Green	*September 14, 1944*
*Michael Harrington	*May 28, 1968*
Thor Heyerdahl	*February 9, 1981*
*James Hilton	*October 1, 1943*
Langston Hughes	*December 8, 1948*
*Aldous Huxley	*July 2, 1943*
Eugene Ionesco	*March 13, 1978*
Christopher Isherwood	*January 10, 1972*
Jerzy Kozinski	*October 14, 1976*
Fulton Lewis III	*May 3, 1963*
Emil Ludwig	*September 14, 1944*
†Thomas Mann	*December 7, 1945*
Dudley Nichols	*October 1, 1943*
Drew Pearson	*March 30, 1960*
James Reston	*July 6, 1960*
Harrison Salisbury	*January 15, 1961*
Carl Sandburg	*November 23, 1958*
*Arthur Schlesinger	*April 26, 1968*
Gilbert Seldes	*October 1, 1943*
†Isaac Bashevis Singer	*May 7, 1979*
C. P. Snow	*December 18, 1960*
Stephen Spender	*March 2, 1977*
Irving Stone	*January 25, 1962*
Arnold Toynbee	*April 1, 1963*
Dalton Trumbo	*October 1, 1943*
Barbara Ward	*April 3, 1957*
Paul Wellman	*January 25, 1956*
John Wexley	*October 1, 1943*

Public Figures

Ansel Adams	*October 12, 1976*
†Jane Addams	*March 31, 1931*
Viscount Alexander of Tunis	*March 21, 1949*
Thomas Hart Benton	*February 26, 1941*
Chester Bowles	*March 11, 1960*

James Henry Breasted	*April 6, 1942*
Benny Bufano	*February 21, 1965*
†Ralph Bunche	*April 17, 1961*
Henry Canby	*March 23, 1932*
James Bryant Conant	*March 25, 1940*
William E. Dodd	*March 17, 1939*
Allen Dulles	*February 28, 1963*
Carl Ebert	*April 21, 1950*
†Albert Einstein	*February 15, 1932*
Hamilton Fish	*April 11, 1949*
Arthur Flemming	*March 28, 1963*
Gerald Ford	*February 16, 1978*
Anna Freud	*April 2, 1959*
J. Paul Getty	*May 7, 1964*
John Glenn	*March 30, 1971*
*Barry Goldwater	*December 13, 1962*
Billy Graham	*October 3, 1952*
William Green	*June 13, 1949*
Mark Hatfield	*January 30, 1964*
Walter Heller	*May 9, 1963*
Hans Hoffman	*October 23, 1957*
Hubert Humphrey	*April 2, 1965*
*Jacob Javits	*October 13, 1960*
John Kennedy	*November 2, 1959*
Alexander Kerensky	*May 7, 1957*
William Knowland	*October 8, 1958*
Phillip F. LaFollette	*March 11, 1941*
Harold Laski	*March 21, 1939*
Louis Leakey	*November 3, 1969*
*Henry Cabot Lodge	*July 13, 1953*
Archibald MacLeish	*March 22, 1943*
Charles Malik	*March 23, 1959*
Jan Masaryk	*March 20, 1959*
*James Francis Cardinal McIntyre	*December 1, 1952*
Pierre Mendes-France	*April 27, 1961*
Wayne Morse	*September 19, 1963*
Chester Nimitz	*March 24, 1950*
Richard Nixon	*March 15, 1962*
Tenzing Norkay	*June 28, 1971*
*Bishop James Pike	*March 4, 1959*
Robert Rauschenberg	*February 26, 1962*
Eddie Rickenbacker	*December 12, 1963*
George Lincoln Rockwell	*May 16, 1967*
Carlos Romulos	*October 1, 1943*
Eleanor Roosevelt	*January 19, 1950*
Robert Schuman	*March 26, 1958*
Fulton Sheen	*June 1, 1934*
Vilhjalmur Stefansson	*February 14, 1938*
Stuart Symington	*February 15, 1960*
Norman Thomas	*November 4, 1960*
Harry Truman	*April 8, 1959*
Stuart Udall	*January 19, 1970*
*Simon Weisenthal	*November 6, 1977*
Ray Lyman Wilbur	*March 24, 1941*
Grant Wood	*February 20, 1940*
Lin Yu Tang	*April 4, 1941*

Orchestras

Academy of St. Martins in the Fields	*October 18, 1981*
Bavarian State Orchestra	*May 11, 1976*
*California Chamber Symphony	*November 6, 1960*
Concertgebouw Orchestra of Amsterdam	*May 7, 1971*
Israeli Chamber Orchestra	*February 3, 1972*
Franz Liszt Chamber Orchestra	*January 11, 1981*
*Japanese Philharmonic	*July 9, 1964*
*Johann Strauss Ensemble	*April 3, 1974*
London Sinfonetta	*October 21, 1976*
*Los Angeles Chamber Symphony	*January 31, 1950*
*Los Angeles Music Festival Orchestra	*April 14, 1950*
*Los Angeles Philharmonic Symphony	*April 15, 1931*
Madrid RTX Symphony	*May 4, 1976*
Meunchen Festival Orchestra	*November 7, 1975*
Milwaukee Symphony	*April 6, 1976*
New American Orchestra	*February 6, 1982*
NDR Symphony Orchestra of Hamburg	*October 12, 1969*
Orchestra San Pietro	*November 20, 1965*
Orchestre de Paris	*May 3, 1970*
Oslo Philharmonic Symphony	*March 1, 1974*
Philadelphia Symphony	*June 4, 1962*
Prague Chamber Orchestra	*January 26, 1975*
Stuttgart Orchestra	*February 18, 1977*
U.S. Marine Band	*October 25, 1966*
*Utah Symphony	*January 19, 1975*
Zurich Chamber Orchestra	*May 2, 1970*

Composers

Leroy Anderson	*March 4, 1935*
Irving Berlin	*September 16, 1944*
Luciano Berio	*April 10, 1964*
Elmer Bernstein	*November 12, 1969*
Charles Wakefield Cadman	*July 21, 1941*
*John Cage	*February 26, 1962*
*Hoagy Charmichael	*January 14, 1946*
*Carlos Chavez	*March 14, 1950*
*Aaron Copland	*April 7, 1948*
*Henry Cowell	*November 5, 1930*
Vernon Duke	*May 27, 1958*
Hanns Eisler	*September 16, 1944*
George Gershwin	*September 28, 1936*
Howard Hansen	*February 8, 1949*
*Roy Harris	*January 21, 1946*
Maurice Jarre	*March 15, 1970*
*Ernst Krenek	*August 1, 1944*
Albert Hay Malotte	*March 2, 1941*
*Johnny Mercer	*February 11, 1944*
*Darius Milhaud	*April 7, 1953*
*Alfred Newman	*May 17, 1961*
Walter Piston	*June 3, 1961*
David Racsin	*September 16, 1944*
Sigmund Romberg	*April 15, 1947*
Miklos Rozsa	*June 3, 1961*
Lalo Schifren	*May 15, 1966*
*Arnold Schoenberg	*March 6, 1937*
William Schuman	*October 7, 1964*
*Karlheinz Stockhausen	*January 16, 1949*
*Igor Stravinsky	*June 16, 1949*
Virgil Thomson	*December 12, 1949*
*David Tudor	*January 16, 1964*
Heitor Villa-Lobos	*January 12, 1954*
*John Vincent	*March 16, 1947*
Sir William Walton	*June 10, 1962*
Ralph Vaughn Williams	*October 20, 1954*

Conductors

Maurice Abravenal	*November 20, 1951*
Modest Altschuler	*February 26, 1936*
*Pierre Boulez	*May 31, 1970*
*Harold Byrns	*January 31, 1950*
*Albert Coates	*February 28, 1940*
*Robert Craft	*May 5, 1966*
Antal Dorati	*February 16, 1944*
*Lawrence Foster	*October 19, 1962*
*Lukas Foss	*May 27, 1954*
Bronislaw Gimpel	*January 26, 1941*
Bernard Haitink	*May 7, 1971*
*Otto Klemperer	*February 1, 1936*
Richard Lert	*November 7, 1945*
James Levine	*December 17, 1975*
Daniel Lewis	*April 12, 1981*
Neville Marriner	*April 18, 1977*
*Mehli Mehta	*November 18, 1964*
*Zubin Mehta	*May 25, 1967*
Eugene Ormandy	*June 4, 1962*
*Jan Popper	*April 21, 1950*
*Charles Previn	*March 21, 1941*
*Artur Rodzinski	*April 15, 1931*
Hans Schmidt-Isserstedt	*October 12, 1961*
Izler Solomon	*January 13, 1953*
Leopold Stokowski	*January 26, 1943*
Henry Svedrofsky	*March 2, 1941*
*Henri Temianka	*November 6, 1960*
*Roger Wagner	*June 10, 1957*
*Alfred Wallenstein	*March 26, 1944*
Bruno Walter	*November 29, 1949*
*Franz Waxman	*June 4, 1948*

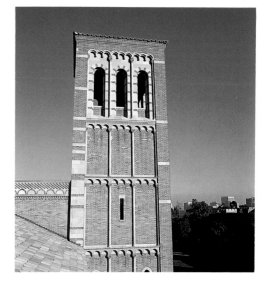

Chamber Groups

Amadeus Quartet	*May 4, 1980*
*Bach Aria Group	*February 5, 1967*
Beaux Arts Trio	*April 24, 1981*
Borodin String Quartet	*June 30, 1965*
*Brandenburg Players	*October 22, 1966*
*Budapest String Quartet	*April 8, 1938*
*Compinsky Trio	*March 30, 1942*
Fires of London	*November 7, 1976*
Gamelan Udan Mas	*November 9, 1956*
*Guarneri String Quartet	*October 17, 1971*
I Musici	*February 2, 1973*
Italian String Quartet	*October 31, 1953*
*Julliard String Quartet	*January 30, 1951*
*Les Menestries	*November 10, 1972*
London String Quartet	*January 11, 1948*
Menuhin Festival Orchestra of London	*November 7, 1975*
Melos Ensemble from Great Britain	*October 16, 1966*
Music From Marlboro	*March 12, 1973*
Netherlands Wind Ensemble	*February 12, 1976*
*New York Chamber Soloists	*March 29, 1963*
*Pro Musica Antigua	*November 8, 1949*
Rostropovich Duo	*March 24, 1980*
*Roth String Quartet	*June 7, 1946*
*Sour Cream	*April 1, 1976*
*Stern-Istomin-Rose Trio	*May 21, 1967*
Tashi	*April 15, 1977*
Trio de Bolzano	*February 1, 1963*
Vienna Concentus	*October 19, 1974*
Von Karajan Organ Ensemble	*February 27, 1966*
Waverly Consort	*December 1, 1972*
Weiner Solisten	*February 17, 1959*
Adolph Weiss Quartet	*November 2, 1938*
Westphalian Kantorei	*April 16, 1961*

Pianists

*Claudio Arrau	*January 25, 1946*
Vladimir Ashkenazy	*December 2, 1965*
Edward Auer	*February 5, 1977*
*Emmanuel Ax	*October 19, 1975*
Gina Bachauer	*March 10, 1974*
*Stefan Bardas	*February 1, 1965*
Daniel Barenboim	*February 15, 1970*
*Alfred Brendel	*May 3, 1974*
John Browning	*April 27, 1974*
*John Cage	*February 26, 1962*
*Robert & Gaby Casadesus	*November 29, 1944*
*Aldo Ciccolini	*February 15, 1975*
*Shura Cherkassky	*November 4, 1961*
*Van Cliburn	*April 3, 1970*
*Bella Davidovich	*November 11, 1979*
*Vasso Devetzi	*January 27, 1974*
*Misha Dichter	*March 14, 1971*
*Alicia de Larrocha	*March 18, 1973*
*Leah Effenbach	*February 19, 1954*
*Phillippe Entrement	*April 10, 1976*
Christoph Eschenbach	*November 8, 1974*
Rudolph Firkusny	*January 23, 1947*
Samson Francois	*November 28, 1961*
*Emil Gilels	*December 13, 1964*
*Jakob Gimpel	*January 26, 1941*
Gary Graffman	*December 6, 1975*
*Horacio Gutierrez	*April 23, 1972*
*Leonid Hambro	*December 4, 1946*
*Joanna Harris	*January 21, 1946*
*Vladimir Horowitz	*March 11, 1943*
*Eugene Istomin	*May 21, 1967*
Jose Iturbi	*May 7, 1966*
Byron Janis	*March 14, 1976*
*Grant Johannesen	*October 22, 1972*
William Kapell	*April 28, 1950*
Constance Keene	*March 21, 1980*
William Kempff	*April 24, 1966*
*Leonid Kogan	*November 18, 1966*
Radu Lapu	*February 14, 1976*
Jacob Lateiner	*February 17, 1979*
Oscar Levant	*June 2, 1958*
Joseph Lhevinne	*April 9, 1942*
*Jerome Lowenthal	*May 10, 1964*
Moura Lympany	*February 13, 1965*
*Witold Malcuyzinski	*January 16, 1951*
Arturo Michelangeli	*November 20, 1966*
*Reid Nibley	*March 3, 1941*
*Minoru Nojima	*March 11, 1978*
John Ogden	*January 19, 1973*
*Leonard Pennario	*October 3, 1965*
*Murray Perahia	*December 1, 1974*
*Daniel Pollack	*January 20, 1962*
Menachem Pressler	*June 4, 1948*
*Andre Previn	*June 10, 1948*

Sviatoslav Richter	*December 17, 1970*
*Joshua Rifkin	*January 20, 1979*
*Artur Rubinstein	*April 4, 1940*
Artur Schnabel	*January 15, 1943*
*Rudolf Serkin	*March 16, 1963*
*Peter Serkin	*December 2, 1973*
Abbey Simon	*February 4, 1978*
*Cutner Solomon	*January 29, 1953*
*Rosalyn Tureck	*November 8, 1963*
*Ilana Vered	*May 19, 1978*
Vronsky and Babin	*March 5, 1967*
*André Watts	*May 17, 1970*
*Alexis Weissenberg	*April 8, 1973*

Organists

William Albright	
*Warren Allen	*February 3, 1932*
Richard Biggs	*April 25, 1941*
*Gaylord Carter	*March 25, 1940*
Palmer Christian	*November 9, 1931*
Joseph Clokey	*July 7, 1937*
Charles Courboin	*November 10, 1932*
David Craighead	*January 26, 1973*
*Catherine Crozier	*January 28, 1972*
Robert Cundick	
*Roland Diggle	*June 30, 1931*
*Ernest Douglas	*July 28, 1931*
Marcel Dupre	*November 8, 1933*
Virgil Fox	*June 11, 1963*
Fernando Germani	
*Harold Gleason	*September 7, 1930*
*Chauncey Haines	*January 31, 1977*
*Thomas Harmon	*June 9, 1969*
Porter Heaps	
Marie Louise Jaquet	
Susan Landale	
*Clarence Mader	*August 4, 1937*
*George Stewart McManus	*April 24, 1931*
*Russell Miles	*June 8, 1936*
Herbert Nannery	*March 4, 1938*
Martin Nearly	
Karol Paukert	*October 7, 1966*
*Lawrence Petran	*July 19, 1939*
Simon Preston	*October 10, 1975*
Peter Pyanyavsky	*May 6, 1976*
*Irene Robertson	*March 18, 1941*
Daniel Roth	
*Alexander Schreiner	*September 19, 1930*
Norman Wright	*June 30, 1942*

Violinists

Mischa Elman	*February 19, 1943*
Zino Francescatti	*December 5, 1968*
*Joseph Fuchs	*May 10, 1964*
*Stephane Grapelli	*March 18, 1976*
Jascha Heifetz	*October 11, 1951*
*Daniel Heifetz	*November 7, 1971*
*Louis Kaufman	*September 17, 1944*
Silvia Marcovici	*February 20, 1977*
*Yehudi Menuhin	*October 25, 1940*
Nathan Milstein	*January 10, 1965*
Erica Morini	*February 21, 1947*
David Oistrakh	*January 5, 1968*
Jean-Luc Ponty	*December 4, 1976*
*Itzak Perlman	*November 9, 1969*
*Ruggiero Ricci	*November 19, 1965*
Eudice Shapiro	*September 17, 1944*
Albert Spalding	*February 15, 1949*
*Tossy Spivakovsky	*November 3, 1956*
*Isaac Stern	*June 3, 1952*
Henryk Szeryng	*November 19, 1972*
*Joseph Szigeti	*February 5, 1942*
Kyung Wha-Chung	*March 16, 1982*
Pinchas Zuckerman	*September 30, 1976*

Harpsichordists

Alice Ehlers	*June 19, 1955*
*Malcolm Hamilton	*November 6, 1966*
Igor Kipnis	*October 30, 1980*
Roland Kirk	*November 22, 1974*
Ralph Kirkpatrick	*October 27, 1973*
*Anthony Newman	*March 23, 1976*
*Rafael Puyana	*November 18, 1966*

Other Prominent Soloists

Jerry Adler, harmonica	*August 7, 1944*
Kalman Bloch, bassoon	*September 15, 1944*
*Julian Bream, lute	*November 10, 1960*
Louise di Tullio, flute	*March 24, 1969*
George Drexler, oboe	*April 21, 1971*
Ziggy Elman, trumpet	*August 7, 1944*
*James Galway, flute	*October 27, 1972*
*Benny Goodman, clarinet	*May 27, 1947*
Lionel Hampton, vibraphone	*March 25, 1940*
Gary Karr, bass viol	*May 16, 1965*
*Sinclair Lott, horn	*May 25, 1934*
*Mitchell Lurie, clarinet	*November 6, 1966*
Virginia Majewski, viola	*September 17, 1944*
Rafael Mendez, trumpet	*May 25, 1954*
*Harry Partch, orchestra	*May 8, 1966*
*William Primrose, viola	*January 6, 1963*
*Jean-Pierre Rampal, flute	*January 23, 1972*
*Dorothy Remson, harp	*November 6, 1966*
*Walter Rubsaman, flute	*March 23, 1945*
Milton Thomas, viola	*October 29, 1972*
Ravi Shankar, sitar	*November 19, 1961*
Nicanor Zabalata, harp	*January 31, 1976*

Guitarists

*Laurindo Almeida	*October 21, 1962*
*Ernesto Bittetti	*November 29, 1975*
Liona Boyd	*February 13, 1982*
Leo Brouwer	*April 19, 1980*
Ray de la Torre	*January 5, 1974*
Paco de Luca	*November 29, 1974*
*Alirio Diaz	*January 31, 1964*
*Oscar Ghiglia	*May 11, 1974*
Jaoa Gilbert	*December 9, 1967*
Turan-Mirza Kamal	*October 27, 1979*
*Leo Kottke	*October 21, 1975*
*Alexandre Lagoya	*November 27, 1977*
*Michael Lorimar	*April 4, 1971*
Vincenzo Macaluso	*December 11, 1981*
*Carlos Montoya	*December 9, 1940*
*Christopher Parkening	*March 6, 1966*
Joe Pass	*October 30, 1976*
Manitas Plaza	*October 17, 1975*
Pascal Roge	*January 9, 1976*
*The Romeros	*December 2, 1962*
*Sabicas	*April 6, 1968*
*Andres Segovia	*February 23, 1967*
*Narcisio Yepes	*November 3, 1973*
Tom Waits	*December 3, 1976*

Vocalists

*Elly Ameling	*March 28, 1976*
*Marian Anderson	*February 18, 1938*
Salvatore Baccaloni	*November 9, 1950*
Janet Baker	*January 12, 1969*
*Richard Dyer Bennett	*June 17, 1959*
Cathy Berberian	*April 10, 1964*
Richard Bonelli	*October 23, 1942*
*Theresa Breganza	*December 1, 1967*
*Grace Bumbry	*January 31, 1971*
*Montserrat Caballé	*March 31, 1974*
Eugene Conley	*May 29, 1951*
Vivian Della Chiesa	*February 20, 1944*
*Alfred Deller	*October 18, 1964*
Victoria de los Angeles	*January 18, 1964*
Guiseppe di Stefano	*February 28, 1950*
Katherine Ferrier	*December 4, 1951*
*Dietrich Fischer-Dieskau	*December 7, 1969*
Maureen Forester	*January 18, 1975*
Nicolai Gedda	*May 16, 1976*
*Igor Gorin	*March 25, 1941*
Donald Gramm	*June 1, 1961*
*Jerome Hines	*November 3, 1942*
*Marilyn Horne	*October 1, 1976*
Mahalia Jackson	*March 22, 1963*
*Helen Jepson	*April 15, 1941*
Howard Keel	*May 17, 1961*
Jan Kiepura	*April 21, 1939*
Alexander Kipnis	*March 10, 1945*
*Dorothy Kirsten	*May 17, 1961*
Militza Korjus	*March 17, 1939*
*Lotte Lehmann	*December 9, 1947*
Nino Martini	*October 27, 1939*
Dorothy Maynor	*January 21, 1944*
Anna Moffo	*March 27, 1966*
Patrice Munsel	*June 2, 1945*
Birgit Nilsson	*March 31, 1971*
*Marni Nixon	*October 22, 1961*
Jessye Norman	*February 13, 1976*
*Luciano Pavarotti	*September 23, 1973*
Jan Peerce	*March 21, 1946*
*Ezio Pinza	*October 11, 1941*
Herman Prey	*February 16, 1969*
*Leontyne Price	*February 14, 1970*
*John Riatt	*March 10, 1944*
*Paul Robeson	*February 25, 1943*
*Bidu Sayao	*December 1, 1939*
*Elizabeth Schwartzkopf	*March 26, 1961*
Cesare Siepi	*October 7, 1980*
Beverly Sills	*April 16, 1972*
*John Charles Thomas	*March 18, 1938*
Jennie Tourel	*March 10, 1961*
Helen Traubel	*April 26, 1943*
Claramae Turner	*May 21, 1966*
*Shirley Verrett-Carter	*June 3, 1960*
Frederica Von Stade	*November 18, 1976*
*Dorothy Warrenskjold	*February 21, 1950*

Cellists

Jacqueline Du Pre	*February 15, 1970*
*Pierre Fournier	*December 11, 1966*
Raya Garbousova	*March 1, 1940*
*Lynn Harrell	*January 30, 1977*
Stephen Kates	*October 10, 1969*
*Yo Yo Ma	*April 17, 1978*
*Zara Nelsova	*May 17, 1978*
Aldo Parisot	*January 16, 1977*
*Kurt Reher	*March 10, 1933*
Gabor Resto	*December 1, 1968*
*Leonard Rose	*February 13, 1966*
*Nathaniel Rosen	*April 11, 1980*
*Mstislav Rostropovich	*April 19, 1969*
*Joseph Schuster	*March 15, 1931*
*Janos Starker	*February 3, 1968*
*Christine Waleska	*January 17, 1971*

Vocal Groups

de Paur Infantry Chorus	*January 11, 1951*
*Don Cossack Chorus	*November 22, 1938*
Gaelic Singers	*February 4, 1961*
Greek Singers	*November 23, 1963*
*Gregg Smith Singers	*June 9, 1963*
Harvard Glee Club	*July 1, 1954*
Jamaican Folk Singers	*May 7, 1972*
Jester Hairston Choir	*May 4, 1958*
Norwegian Boys' Choir	*October 9, 1975*
*Roger Wagner Chorale	*April 14, 1950*
Rutgers Glee Club	*April 1, 1960*
Swingle Singers	*November 5, 1965*
The Gay Tyroliers	*October 26, 1954*
The Weavers	*April 9, 1960*
*Vienna Boys' Choir	*February 4, 1937*
Westminster Chorus	*February 12, 1940*

Opera

The Bartered Bride	*April 21, 1950*
The Beggar's Opera	*May 24, 1950*
The Bewitched	*January 4, 1975*
*Candide	*October 11, 1951*
Cosi Fan Tutti	*November 9, 1948*
Eugen Onegin	*June 2, 1967*
Falstaff	*May 21, 1971*
*Faust	*December 18, 1940*
Forever Rembrandt	*January 16, 1955*
The Good Soldier Schweik	*October 19, 1966*
*Hansel and Gretel	*April 9, 1938*
Idomeneo	*May 12, 1974*
The Impressario	*January 16, 1955*
I Pagliacci	*September 24, 1940*
Jenufa	*May 4, 1974*
*La Traviata	*November 19, 1943*
Les Huguenots	*May 23, 1969*
L'Histoire du Soldat	*June 16, 1949*
The Marriage of Figaro	*June 9, 1949*
Mavra	*June 5, 1953*
The Medium	*March 10, 1954*
The Mines of Sulphur	*June 5, 1970*
Orpheus	*May 22, 1954*
The Passion of Oedipus	*November 8, 1968*
Rigoletto	*March 17, 1944*
The Sinking of the Titanic	*November 14, 1980*
Turandot	*June 3, 1957*

Dance Companies

**African Dancers	March 6, 1954
Alvin Ailey Dancers	April 12, 1964
*Alvin Nikolais	February 7, 1970
*Aman Dancers	March 14, 1972
*Ann Halprin	May 5, 1949
Avaz Dance Company	May 22, 1982
Ballet Rambert	November 19, 1982
Ballet Russe	November 10, 1946
*Ballet Theatre	February 16, 1944
*Ballet Trockadero	October 24, 1976
*Bayanian Dancers	September 29, 1961
*Bejart Ballet	February 2, 1974
*Bella Lewitzky	January 24, 1976
Carmen de Lavallade	January 15, 1967
*Ceylon National Dancers	October 17, 1958
Classical Khmer Ballet	November 5, 1971
Dance Theater of Harlem	June 10, 1977
Danzas Venezuela	October 13, 1968
*Dan Wagoner Dance	October 22, 1976
*Devi Dja Balinese Dancers	April 26, 1940
*Eliot Feld Ballet	February 11, 1977
*Erik Hawkins Dancers	October 31, 1964
*Escudero	November 4, 1960
Fiesta Mexicana	July 29, 1966
Frula	May 11, 1968
Glen Tetley	April 19, 1968
Grand Ballet Classique de France	October 30, 1965
Haitian Dance Company	March 24, 1963
Hanya Holm	November 10, 1938
Harkness Ballet	January 20, 1970
Humphrey and Weidman	March 15, 1938
*Jean Erdman	February 28, 1964
Jose Greco	January 27, 1967
*Jose Limon	February 22, 1961
*Korean Dancers	March 10, 1964
La Argentina	December 9, 1940
Lar Lubovitch Dance Company	May 19, 1973
Les Grand Ballets Canadiens	February 19, 1966
*Lester Horton Dance Group	April 6, 1938
Lotte Goslar	November 5, 1957
Lucas Hoving	April 30, 1966
Malinese Dancers	November 26, 1972
*Martha Graham	October 3, 1966
Meredith Monk	April 7, 1979
*Merce Cunningham	April 21, 1948
*Murray Louis Dance Company	March 26, 1974
*National Ballet of Canada	January 22, 1971
National Ballet of Washington	February 22, 1970
Oakland Ballet	April 2, 1981
Okinawa Dance Company	October 10, 1981
Paul Draper	February 10, 1956
*Paul Taylor Dancers	October 27, 1963
*Pennsylvania Ballet	April 5, 1974
*Pilobolus Dance Company	April 26, 1976
Pirin Folk Ensemble	October 14, 1982
Robert Joffrey Ballet	February 1, 1964
Royal Winnipeg Ballet	October 16, 1971
*Rudy Perez Dance Company	January 29, 1972
*San Francisco Ballet	December 16, 1957
Sierra Leone National Dance Company	January 22, 1972
Tap II	December 20, 1979
Toy Box Ballet	June 13, 1959
Tradisches Ballet	December 5, 1980
Trudi Schoop	February 18, 1939
Twyla Tharp	February 9, 1978
Utah Repertory Dance Company	April 19, 1976
Viola Farber	January 26, 1974
Yugoslavian Dancers	December 7, 1973

Dancers

Alicia Alonso	February 22, 1945
Lucia Chase	February 22, 1945
Antoinette Cobos	June 16, 1949
Alexandra Danilova	October 28, 1954
*Anton Dolin	February 21, 1946
Katherine Dunham	December 9, 1941
*Angna Enters	March 17, 1949
*Saida Gerrard	January 7, 1961
Rosella Hightower	February 22, 1945
Nora Kaye	February 16, 1944
Michael Kidd	February 21, 1946
John Kriza	February 22, 1945
Harold Liang	February 16, 1944
Eugene Loring	April 3, 1960
*Alicia Markova	February 21, 1946
Carmen Maracci	February 17, 1949
Maria Tallchief	February 22, 1945
*Tamara Toumanova	February 22, 1945
Anthony Tudor	February 16, 1944

Theater Performers

Steve Allen	*January 21, 1961*
Lew Ayres	*October 16, 1960*
Frank Baxter	*November 23, 1958*
Edgar Bergen	*March 26, 1942*
Charles Boyer	*June 6, 1946*
Victor Borge	*May 9, 1947*
*Joe E. Brown	*September 27, 1933*
*Francis X. Bushman	*December 5, 1929*
Carol Burnett	*May 6, 1954*
George Burns	*November 4, 1982*
Morris Carnovsky	*March 17, 1964*
Johnny Carson	*June 2, 1977*
Charles Coburn	*May 9, 1947*
Nat King Cole	*March 2, 1955*
Ethel Barrymore Colt	*October 21, 1960*
Bill Cosby	*March 15, 1970*
Joseph Cotton	*June 5, 1961*
Tony Curtis	*October 29, 1951*
Jimmy Durante	*October 29, 1941*
Gus Edwards	*September 25, 1929*
Nina Foch	*February 7, 1965*
Vittorio Gassman	*March 5, 1966*
Sir John Gielgud	*December 6, 1958*
Sir Tyrone Guthrie	*December 11, 1964*
Charlton Heston	*December 21, 1969*
*Hal Holbrook	*May 7, 1963*
Burton Holmes	*May 31, 1951*
Bob Hope	*May 28, 1981*
*John Houseman	*February 25, 1964*
Gene Kelly	*May 9, 1965*
*Claude Kipnis	*April 21, 1968*
Burt Lancaster	*October 5, 1960*
Elsa Lancaster	*October 2, 1960*
Charles Laughton	*May 25, 1961*
Jerry Lewis	*October 30, 1951*
*Dwight Long	*November 9, 1940*
*Marais and Miranda	*March 20, 1965*
*Marcel Marceau	*March 15, 1968*
Dean Martin	*October 30, 1951*
Marilyn Monroe	*November 21, 1952*
Max Morath	*July 18, 1974*
*Vincent Price	*June 6, 1946*
Basil Rathbone	*November 10, 1943*
Ronald Reagan	*October 29, 1941*
Sir Michael Redgrave	*December 4, 1967*
Mickey Rooney	*March 6, 1937*
Ritz Brothers	*October 28, 1940*
Anna Russell	*March 14, 1964*
Joseph Schildkraut	*June 13, 1960*
Phil Silvers	*October 29, 1941*
*Frank Sinatra	*June 10, 1967*
*Cornelia Otis Skinner	*February 3, 1950*
Lee Strasburg	*October 7, 1967*
*Theater of the Deaf	*November 17, 1974*
Michael Todd	*March 17, 1958*

Ben Vereen	*December 18, 1982*
Allan Villiers	*March 16, 1937*
Sam Wanamaker	*June 11, 1948*
*Doodles Weaver	*March 15, 1937*
Orson Welles	*May 16, 1940*
Oscar Werner	*March 20, 1967*
*Emlyn Williams	*March 5, 1965*
William Windom	*December 3, 1972*
Dame May Whitty	*January 29, 1945*
Jane Wyman	*October 29, 1941*
*Vera Zorina	*June 11, 1948*

Shakespearean Plays

Hamlet	*October 22, 1970*
*Henry IV, Part I	*April 10, 1957*
Julius Caesar	*March 9, 1938*
*Love's Labour's Lost	*November 13, 1940*
Macbeth	*November 29, 1950*
Merchant of Venice	*December 17, 1952*
Merry Wives of Windsor	*December 5, 1929*
Midsummer Night's Dream	*May 28, 1952*
*Much Ado About Nothing	*November 19, 1958*
Richard II	*November 14, 1961*
Richard III	*December 2, 1929*
*Romeo and Juliet	*April 20, 1955*
*The Tempest	*April 12, 1939*
Twelfth Night	*December 8, 1933*

Greek Plays

Agamemnon	*May 19, 1932*
Alcestis	*May 22, 1936*
Antigone	*May 21, 1937*
Choephoroe	*May 25, 1933*
Electra	*January 19, 1943*
Iphigenia in Taurus	*May 22, 1930*
Lysistrata	*November 3, 1948*
Medea	*May 20, 1931*
*Oedipus Rex	*May 24, 1934*
The Eumenides	*May 25, 1934*
*Trojan Women	*November 3, 1948*

Other Plays

*Alice in Wonderland	December 2, 1941
Ah! Wilderness	October 7, 1941
The Barretts of Wimpole Street	July 27, 1931
The Beaux Strategem	July 21, 1932
Berkeley Square	November 5, 1931
Caesar and Cleopatra	May 9, 1956
*Cyrano de Bergerac	April 4, 1930
Dr. Faustus	March 14, 1941
An Enemy of the People	January 8, 1941
Elizabeth the Queen	April 4, 1934
Ethan Frome	July 28, 1937
Everyman	June 7, 1941
*Faust	May 6, 1932

Ghosts	February 24, 1943
Knickerbocker Holiday	April 23, 1941
The Knight of the Burning Pestle	May 14, 1942
Le Bourgeois Gentilhomme	November 16, 1939
Life With Father	March 26, 1940
Marco's Millions	March 25, 1931
Men in White	April 14, 1937
Mourning Becomes Electra	July 26, 1932
Of Mice and Men	July 27, 1949
*Of Thee I Sing	July 12, 1932
*Once in a Lifetime	April 7, 1932
*Our Town	May 22, 1940
*The Playboy of the Western World	July 25, 1933
*Saint Joan	April 20, 1949
*She Stoops to Conquer	December 7, 1960
Stage Door	March 16, 1938
The Children's Hour	March 22, 1937
*The Importance of Being Earnest	October 15, 1940
The Rivals	November 12, 1941
*The Three Sisters	December 1, 1944
Tonight at 8:30	July 26, 1945
Volpone	December 11, 1957
*Yellow Jack	April 3, 1935

Films

A Night at the Opera	March 12, 1965
*A Nous La Liberte	September 21, 1960
Bicycle Thieves	March 10, 1954
Cavalcade	November 29, 1938
The Captain from Koepenick	November 16, 1960
The Children of Paradise	July 18, 1961
Citizen Kane	December 7, 1967
Der Rosenkavalier	June 6, 1963
Dr. Zhivago	April 9, 1975
Eugen Onegin	February 5, 1960
The Gold Rush	June 24, 1961
Gone with the Wind	April 23, 1975
*The Grand Illusion	April 18, 1939
The Grapes of Wrath	March 19, 1964
The Great Train Robbery	September 28, 1937
Hamlet	October 1, 1964
High Noon	November 9, 1967
The Jazz Singer	November 29, 1937
Juliet of the Spirits	October 15, 1969
Intolerance	October 26, 1937
Lola	June 27, 1968
M	August 24, 1962
Marty	February 21, 1961
Nanook of the North	July 7, 1962
*Open City	June 3, 1946
Queen Christina	November 18, 1965
*The Red Shoes	February 27, 1958
The River	October 14, 1940
San Pietro	October 24, 1961
Sunset Boulevard	August 10, 1962
Stagecoach	December 7, 1967
*The Treasure of Sierra Madre	May 24, 1955
Vampyr	January 13, 1962

Pop Artists and Groups

*Cannonball Adderly	October 29, 1966
*Akiyoshi-Tabackin Big Band	July 15, 1977
Laurie Anderson	May 10, 1982
Louis Armstrong Orchestra	November 16, 1965
Joan Baez	March 24, 1961
Count Basie Band	September 20, 1977
Harry Belafonte	November 17, 1964
Willie Bobo	February 4, 1969
*Les Brown	June 6, 1965
*Dave Brubeck	September 23, 1957
The Chieftans	November 20, 1975
Christy Minstrels	March 4, 1963
Leonard Cohen and the Army	November 14, 1970
Crosby and Nash	October 11, 1971
*Miles Davis Quintet	September 28, 1963
*Jimmy Dorsey's Band	May 29, 1936
Bob Dylan	December 6, 1964
Duke Ellington's Orchestra	January 21, 1937
Ella Fitzgerald	December 9, 1961
Dizzy Gillespie	November 3, 1962
*Arlo Guthrie	January 10, 1969
Woody Herman	January 29, 1977
Earl Hines	January 29, 1978
Paul Horn Quintet	May 15, 1966
Burl Ives	March 25, 1950
*Al Jarreau	December 16, 1979
Jefferson Starship	February 14, 1980
Elton John	December 6, 1970
Stan Kenton	June 1, 1966
*B. B. King	May 16, 1972
Kris Kristofferson	May 27, 1971
Gene Krupa's Band	February 20, 1939
*Cleo Laine and John Dankworth	October 15, 1974
*Tom Lehrer	October 30, 1958
Miriam Makeba	January 12, 1964
Manhattan Transfer	December 6, 1979
*Modern Jazz Quintet	September 26, 1964
Thelonius Monk Quintet	October 17, 1974
*Holly Near	May 17, 1981
Randy Newman	October 23, 1971
Nitty Gritty Dirt Band	April 11, 1975
*Odetta	February 9, 1961
*Preservation Hall Jazz	July 29, 1969
The Ramones	October 28, 1979

*Linda Ronstadt	October 25, 1969
Gil Scott-Heron	February 25, 1982
*Pete Seeger	May 3, 1963
Artie Shaw's Band	May 22, 1939
*George Shearing	October 8, 1956
Simon and Garfunkle	March 30, 1968
*Tower of Power	February 1, 1978

Rudy Vallee's Orchestra	December 11, 1942
Sarah Vaughn	April 14, 1977
Fred Waring's Pennsylvanians	April 14, 1930
*Doc Watson	May 7, 1974
Margaret Whiting	May 14, 1948
*Paul Winter Consort	July 18, 1970
*Frank Zappa	September 17, 1975

Royce Hall 170 Production

The process of converting Royce Hall room #170 into a functioning theater where public performances were scheduled started as early as 1942. Theater 170 served admirably as a performance venue during the World War II years permitting theater activity on campus to survive without the investment of large stage productions which the use of Royce Hall Auditorium would require. In the Fall of 1947, with the beginning of the newly approved Department of Theater Arts, the production of *The Wanhope Building* initiated Theater 170 as the major performing venue of the Department until its permanent home in Macgowan Hall was built. Here is a list of the productions which were performed in that theater.

1942	*Altruism*
1943	*Ghosts*
1943	*Goodbye Again*
1943	*Volpone*
1943	*Family Portrait*
1943	*Anatol*
1944	*The Male Animal*
1944	*Yellow Jacket*
1944	*Alison's House*
1944	*Dover Road*
1944	*Scenes from 5 comedies*
1946	*Can Spring Be Far Behind?*
1946	*Displaced Person*
1946	*Man and Superman*
1947	*The Great God Brown*
1947	*Hay Fever*
1947	*The Frogs*
1947	*Four one-act plays*
1947	*Short story adaptations*
1947	*The Wanhope Building*
1947	*Richard II*
1947	*The Play's the Thing*
1948	*The White Steed*
1948	*The Suspect*
1948	*Verily I Do*
1948	*Thunder Rock*
1948	*Periphery*
1948	*Twelfth Night*
1949	*The Hasty Heart*
1949	*The Seagull*
1949	*Ah! Wilderness*
1949	*Portrait in Black*
1949	*Roadside*
1949	*The Miser*
1950	*Blithe Spirit*
1950	*He Who Gets Slapped*
1950	*All My Sons*
1950	*Papa Is All*
1950	*Machinal*
1950	*Yellow Jacket*
1951	*The Late Christopher Bean*
1951	*The Circle*

1951	*The Green Cockatoo*
1951	*Literature*
1951	*Candida*
1951	*House in a Sea*
1952	*Two Blind Mice*
1952	*Lower Depths*
1952	*The Philadelphia Story*
1952	*The Truth About Blayds*
1952	*Even the Gods*
1953	*The Wedding Present*
1953	*Front Page*
1953	*An Ideal Husband*
1953	*Hedda Gabler*
1953	*Tobias and the Angel*
1954	*The Broken Stairway*
1954	*Lady Precious Stream*
1954	*The Happy Time*
1954	*Love of Four Colonels*
1955	*Dragon By Moonshine*
1955	*Miss Julia*
1955	*The Stronger*
1955	*Payment Deferred*
1955	*Allegro*
1956	*Bell, Book and Candle*
1956	*Lady of the Dawn*
1956	*On Borrowed Time*
1956	*The Crucible*
1957	*The Glass Menagerie*
1957	*The Playboy of the Western World*
1957	*The Lady's Not for Burning*
1957	*Detective Story*
1957	*The Snob*
1958	*The Country Girl*
1958	*Teach Me How to Cry*
1958	*The Tallest Baby on the River*
1959	*Yes My Lord*
1959	*Heidi*
1959	*Uncle Vanya*
1959	*Portrait in Greasepaint*
1959	*Yankee Don't Go Home*
1960	*Hunters and the Henwife*
1960	*The Cocktail Party*
1960	*The Good Woman of Setzuan*
1960	*Island of Goats*
1960	*She Stoops to Conquer*
1961	*The Red Shoes*
1961	*The Just Assassins*
1961	*Antigone*
1961	*Forty Five Minutes From Broadway*
1961	*Not for Children*
1961	*Richard II*
1961	*The Bashful Genius*
1962	*Puddin' Tame*
1962	*Clerembard*
1962	*Ah Sin*
1962	*Light of Love*
1962	*You Never Can Tell*
1962	*A Country Scandal*
1962	*Pocatan*

Discography

The following is a listing of the recordings made in Royce Hall Auditorium. The acoustical properties of the auditorium have always been admired by recording engineers.

Five Centuries of Men's Choral Music
UCLA Glee Club, Donn Weiss, Director
An Everest Record Production: #6164

Charpentier: *Magnificat*
Carissimi: *Plorate, Filii, Israel*
Bartok: *Three Slovak folksongs*
Da Nola: *Are All the Ladies Deaf?*
Dowland: *Come Again, Sweet Love*
Schubert: *Widerspruch*
Dvorak: *Maegdlein Im Walde*
Dvorak: *Gram*

Thomas Harmon Plays American Organ Music
   of Three Centuries
Orion Master Recordings, Inc.: ORS 76255
Side II on the Royce Hall Skinner Organ

Sowerby: *Prelude on "The King's Majesty"*
Paine: *Prelude in D Flat Major, Op. 19, No. 1*
Parker: *Fugue in C Minor, Op. 36, No. 3*
Farnum: *Toccata on "O Filii et Filiae"*

Starlight Concert
The Hollywood Bowl Symphony Orchestra,
   Carmen Dragon, Conductor
Capitol Records, Inc.: DP 8276 (recorded 1953,
   released 1954)

Sibelius: *Finlandia*
Rimsky-Korsakov: *Flight of the Bumblebee*
von Weber: *Invitation to the Dance*
Tchaikovsky: *None But the Lonely Heart*
Debussy: *Clair de Lune*
Sibelius: *Valse Triste*
Brahms: *Hungarian Dance No. 5*
Elgar: *Pomp and Circumstance March No. 1*

Echoes of Space
The Hollywood Bowl Symphony Orchestra,
   Carmen Dragon, Conductor
Capitol Records, Inc.: DP 8275 (recorded 1953,
   released 1954)

Chabrier: *Espana*
da Falla: *Ritual Fire Dance*
Granados: *Intermezzo from "Goyescas"*
Lecuona: *Andalucia*
Gade: *Jalousie*
Ponce: *Estrellita*
Lecuona: *Malaguena*
Padilla: *El Relicario*

Jazz Rolls Royce
Howard Rumsey and the Lighthouse All Stars
Omega Record Company: OSL 5 (Recorded on
October 28, 1957 during the Homecoming Show
at UCLA, Royce Hall Auditorium)

Strike Up the Band
Prelude to the Queen
The Clowns' Dance
Coop Salutes "Co-op"
Bruinville, My Bruinville
Mambo del Quado

All songs except *Strike Up the Band* were written
by Bob Cooper. Album has a photograph of a Rolls
Royce in front of Royce Hall with Skip Keyzers,
Homecoming Chairman and John Brown, Program
Chairman.

Cleo Laine and John Dankworth
Video tape of entire special production on
October 15, 1974.
No other commercial release except on network
television.

Tron, Walt Disney Productions, score of the film
Music by Wendy Carlos
Released by Buena Vista Distributing Company,
Inc.: CBS 37782
Portions of score recorded in Royce Hall by the
UCLA Chorus conducted by Donn Weiss. 1982.

Jazz Alive series, National Public Radio
Released for broadcast only on NPR,
November 1981.
Recorded on September 26, 1981.

   Carmen McRae and Trio
   Benny Carter Quintet
   Central Avenue Breakdown All Stars
      Red Callender   John Collins
      Buster Cooper   Lawrence Marable
      Marshall Royal   Zoot Sims
      Billy Taylor   Snooky Young
Recorded on September 27, 1981
   Gerald Wilson Orchestra

   Dexter Gordon
   Zoot Sims
   Art Pepper
   Harold Land
   Ray Brown
   Billy Higgens
Series produced by Tim Owens

Orchestral Favorites
Frank Zappa
Discreet Records: DSK 2294 (released May 10, 1979)

Strictly Genteel
Pedro's Dowry
Naval Aviation in Art?
Duke of Prunes
Bogus Pomp

The eleven-year series of recordings made by the Los Angeles Philharmonic Symphony Orchestra under the London Records (Decca) label began in 1967 and extended to 1978. All of the albums recorded in this period, unless otherwise noted, were conducted by Zubin Mehta.

1967
Schoenberg, *Verklarte Nacht, Op. 4* **CS 6552**
Scriabin, *The Poem of Ecstasy*

Tchaikovsky, *Symphony No. 4 in F Minor, Op. 36* **CS 6553**

Stravinsky, *Petroushka* **CS 6554**
Stravinsky, *Circus Polka*

Mussorgsky-Ravel, *Pictures at an Exhibition* (side two) **CS 6559**

1968
Strauss, *Ein Heldenleben, Op. 40* **CS 6608**

Strauss, *Also Sprach Zarathustra, Op. 30* **CS 6609**

1969
Schoenberg, *Chamber Symphony, Op. 9* **CS 6612**
Schoenberg, *Variations, Op. 31*

Copland, *Lincoln Portrait* (with Gregory Peck) **CS 6613**
Kraft, *Contextures: Riots—Decade '60, Concerto for Percussion*

1970
Strauss, *Sinfonia Domestica, Op. 53* **CS 6663**

Stravinsky, *La Sacre du Printemps* **CS 6664**
Stravinsky, *Eight Instrumental Miniatures for Fifteen Players*

Tchaikovsky, *Overture Sollnnelle 1812, Op. 49* **CS 6670**
Tchaikovsky, *Fantasy Overture— Romeo and Juliet*

1971
Saint-Saens, *Symphony No. 3 in C Minor, Op. 78* **CS 6680**
Bruckner, *Symphony No. 4 in E Flat Major*

Ravel, *Daphnis and Chloe, 2nd Suite* **CS 6698**
Ravel, *Ma Mere L'Oye*
Ravel, *La Valse*

Holst, *The Planets—Suite* **CS 6734**

1972
Liszt, *The Battle of the Huns, Symphonic Poem, No. 11* **CS 6738**
Liszt, *Orpheus, Symphonic Poem, No. 4*
Liszt, *Mazeppa, Symphonic Poem, No. 6*

Varese, *Arcana* **CS 6752**
Varese, *Integrales*
Varese, *Ionisation*

1973
Ives, *Symphony No. 1* **CS 6816**
Elgar, *Enigma Variations, Op. 36*

Strauss, *Also Sprach Zarathustra* **CS 6823**
Holst, *The Planets*
Ravel, *The Bolero*
Bizet, *Carmen—Prelude to Act One*

Von Suppe, *Poet and Peasant Overture*
Tchaikovsky, *1812 Overture*
(Previously recorded and released)

1974
Bruckner, *Symphony No. 8 in C Minor* **CSA 2237**

Neilson, *Symphony No. 4* **CS 6848**

Strauss, *Don Quixote* **CS 6849**

Mozart, *Le Nozze di Figaro Overture* **CS 6858**
Strauss, J., *Die Fledermaus Overture*
Rossini, *La Gazza Ladra Overture*
Weber, *Der Frieschutz Overture*
Wagner, *Rienzi Overture*

Beethoven, *Egmont Overture, Op. 84* **CS 6870**
Beethoven, *Symphony No. 7 in A Major, Op. 92*

1975
Bernstein, *Candide Overture* **CS 2246**
Copland, *Appalachian Spring*
Ives, *Symphony No. 2*
Ives, *Decoration Day*
Schuman, *Variations on "America"*
Gershwin, *An American in Paris*

Rimsky-Korsakov, *Scheherazade* **CS 6950**

Dvorak, *Symphony No. 8* **CS 6979**
Dvorak, *Wood Dove*

Dvorak, *Symphony No. 9* **CS 6980**
Dvorak, *Carnival Overture*

1976
Mahler, *Symphony No. 5* **CS 2248**
Mahler, *Symphony No. 10*
Mahler, *Adagio*

Copland, *Appalachian Spring (Suite)* **CS 7031**
Bernstein, *Candide Overture*
Gershwin, *An American in Paris*

1976
Ravel, *Bolero* **CS 7132**
Bizet, *Carmen Prelude, Act I and Act IV*
Verdi, *Forza del Destino Overture*
Von Suppe, *Poet and Peasant Overture*

1977
Verdi, *Pezzi sacri* (with Los Angeles   26178
    Master Chorale)

Strauss, *Alpensinfonie*   CS 8691

Haydn, *Trumpet Concerto* (Stevens)   CS 8967
Vivaldi, *Piccolo Concerto,*
    in A, P. 231 (Zentner)
Von Weber, *Clarinet Concerto,*
    Op. 26 (Zukovsky)
Wieniawski, *Polonaise de Concert, Op. 4* (Dicterow)
Weiniawski, *Scherzo-Tarantelle,*
    Op. 16 for violin (Dicterow)
(Philharmonic Soloists)
Williams, *Suites from* Star Wars *and*
    Close Encounters of the Third Kind

Additionally, during 1977, the orchestra recorded
under the CBS Records label, conducted by Michael
Tilson Thomas:
Bartok, *Violin Concerto No. 2*   M 35156
    (Pinchas Zukerman, Violin)

Bruch, *Violin Concerto No. 1*   M 35132
Lalo, Symphonie Espagnole
    (Pinchas Zukerman, Violin)

Tchaikovsky, *Suite No. 3*   M 35124

Under the New World records label, conducted by
Calvin Simmons, they recorded
Carpenter, *Krazy Kat*   228
Gilbert, *Dance in Place Congo*
Powell, *Rhapsodie Negre*
    (Zita Carno, Piano)

1978
Beethoven, *Piano Concerto No. 5*   CS 7121
    (Alicia de Larrocha, Piano)

Mahler, *Symphony No. 3*   CS 2249
    (Maureen Forrester, Contralto,
    Women of the Roger Wagner
    Chorale, California Boys' Choir)

1978
Mahler, *Ruckert Lieder*   26578
Mahler, *Lieder eines Fahrenden*
    Gesellen (Marilyn Horne, Soprano)

In 1978, under the CBS Records label, again con-
ducted by Michael Tilson Thomas, they recorded
Prokofiev, *Lt. Kije Suite*
Prokofiev, *The Love of*
    Three Oranges Suite

Respighi, *Fountains of Rome*   M 35846
Respighi, *Roman Festivals*

1979
In 1979, under the CBS Records label, conducted by
Jesus Lopez-Cobos, they recorded
Chabrier, *Espana*
De Falla, *Three Cornered Hat,*
    Suites No. 1 and 2
Rimsky-Korsakov, *Capriccio Espagnol*

Led by conductor Charles Dutoit, they recorded
Tchaikovsky, *Piano Concerto No. 1*
    in B Flat, Op. 23
    (Myung-Whun Chung, Piano)
Tchaikovsky, *Rococo Variations, Op. 33*
    (Myung-Wha Chung, Cello)

1981
In 1981, led by their new permanent conductor,
Carlo Maria Giulini, for the Deutsche Grammaphon
label, they recorded
Beethoven, *Symphony No. 5*   DG 2532049

Brahms, *Symphony No. 1*   DG 2532056

Schumann, *Manfred Overture*   DG 2532040

Quotations from the third floor loggia ceiling decoration.

Petrarch: "I have constantly striven to place myself in spirit in other ages."

Loyola: "Novices shall love poverty and strive after righteousness."

Abelard: "It is through doubt we come to investigation and through investigation to the truth."

Melanchthon: "For the truths of religion and duty can be perceived only by minds soundly trained by the practice of past ages."

Christ: "A new commandment I give unto you . . ."

Plato: "He will look at the city which is within him."

Socrates: "An unexamined life is not fit to be lived by any man."

Aristotle: "Justice is the bond of men in states."

Kant: "So act as to treat humanity in every case as an end: never as a means only."

Einstein: "The only justification for our concepts and system of concepts is that they serve to represent the complex of our experience."

Darwin: "The great point is to give up the immutability of specific forms."

Eliot: "There is but one road upward—more education and wiser."

Great practitioners: Painted at the base of the twelve medieval professions on the ceiling of the first floor loggia.

Chemistry: Mendeleeff, Lavoisier, Avogadro, Cannizzaro, Arrhenius

Graphic Art: Phidias, Giotto, Leonardo, Michelangelo, Rembrandt, Titian

Literature/Drama: Homer, Sophocles, Virgil, Dante, Montaigne, Cervantes, Shakespeare

History: Herodotus, Thucydides, Tacitus, Gibbon, Guizot, Ranke, Macaulay

Education: Socrates, Plato, Quintilian, Petrarch, Melanchthon, Loyola, Locke, Rousseau

Mathematics: Gauss, Euclid, Newton, Euler, Cauchy, Lagrange, Descartes, Archimedes, Klein, Poincare

Music: Palestrina, Bach, Beethoven, Wagner, Brahms, Verdi, Franck, Debussy, Tschaikowsky

Philosophy: Socrates, Plato, Aristotle, Aquinas, Descartes, Spinoza, Locke, Hume, Kant, Hegel

Physics: Galvan, Newton, Faraday, Kelvin, Maxwell, Thomson

Language: Socrates, Cicero, Dante, Chaucer, Hume, Grimm, Boileau

Astronomy: Newton, Copernicus, Galileo, Kepler, Einstein, Hipparchus, Herschel, Kirckhoff, Tycho

Biology: Linnaeus, Darwin, Mendel, Pasteur, Harvey, Lamarck, Galton, Vesalius, Muller, Lister

PHOTO CREDITS

California Historical Society, 71R
California Monthly, 17
Phillip Channing, 81L
Tom Feldman, 48B, 50, 52, 59, 61, 99C
John Gaylord, dust cover, title page, 3, 5, 20, 21, 23, 25C, 29, 30, 32, 51, 72, 77, 79, 80, 81R, 82, 83L, 84, 86, 93, 94, 95, 96A, 97C/R, 100R, 102, 103, 104C/R, 105, 106R, 107, 108L, 109, 110L
F. M. Godfrey: *Italian Architecture Up to 1750,* Page 28A
Harvard University Archives, 2, 35
Thelner Hoover, 14, 37R
John Jackson, 38R
James Klain, 68, 69
Richard Kent Nystrom, 13L/R
David Palmer, 101L
Otto Rothschild, 62
Pete Saloutos, 24, 112
Steven Sann, 41, 49R
Norman Schindler, 11R, 25L, 31, 34, 36, 39, 40 70, 96B, 97L, 98, 99L/R, 100L, 101R, 104L, 106L
Spence Air Photos, 9, 12, 22, 88, 90
Howard Tribe, 26, 27, 28B, 53R, 56B, 75, 76, 78, 83R, 101C, 108R, 110R
Stan Troutman, 60
UCLA Alumni Association, 19LR, 38L, 45
UCLA Campus Activities Service Office, 48A, 55, 56A, 63
UCLA Library/Special Collections, 15
UCLA Library/University Archives, 8, 10, 11L, 13C, 18, 19UL, 19UR, 19LL, 42LL, 44, 46, 54, 57, 58, 65, 66, 67L, 71L, 87, 89, 91
UCLA Planning Office, 92
UCLA Southern Campus, end sheet, 37L, 42UL, 42R, 43, 47, 49L, 53L, 64, 67R

Location symbols: A: above; B: below; L: left; C: center; R: right; UL: upper left; UR: upper right; LL: lower left; LR: lower right

CATALOG CREDITS

Design: Jack Carter
Production Art: Roberta Roberts
Produced by:
UCLA Publication Services Department
Publication Coordinator: Judy Hale
Typesetting: Capco, Los Angeles
Text Type: Baskerville 12/14
Color separations, printing, and binding: Dai Nippon Printing Company
5000 Copies
Printed in Japan